CHILBLAINS AND CHITTERLINGS

A Working Class Childhood in 1960s Birmingham

Dawn Fallon

NOTE

**FOR PHOTOS (many in full colour) AND LINKS
RELATED TO THIS MEMOIR - PLEASE VISIT
DAWN FALLON AUTHOR - BLOG**

DEDICATED TO MY PARENTS AND GRANDPARENTS

"Forever is composed of nows..."

EMILY DICKINSON

CONTENTS

PROLOGUE

I was nearly never born.

But before I tell the tale relating to that issue, I should explain that this memoir begins in 2013 with some of my experiences as a hotel pianist in Devon.

Then, as the world emerged from the pandemic in 2020, childhood memories came flooding back as I drove to work one evening, retreating in time, urging me to write about times gone by…

1. BACK TO THE FUTURE

I don't know what made me do it.

I'd been playing the piano during dinner every Saturday night at a hotel near Babbacombe in Devon for two years, but I had never considered doing it before.

But it came to me out of the blue: Why not check the hotel's Trip Advisor reviews and see if anyone mentions how amazing the pianist is?

I cherished my position as a hotel pianist, although securing the role had proved challenging. It began when I'd reinvented myself in my early 50s after a prolonged period of glumness —my Eeyore years, as I call them—where I'd felt drawn back to playing the piano. It had helped to soothe away the black dog of depression. So, I was feeling rather pleased with my transformation.

Moreover, a hotel restaurant is such a convivial place to work. A happy atmosphere pervades the dining room as guests wine and dine, natter, chatter, and laugh the evening away, along with the occasional *POP!* of a champagne cork in the background. *Such a happy sound.*

But that wasn't the only thing. I'd participated in a "talent show" aboard the Queen Mary 2 in 2011, performing Bach on the ballroom's fabulous Steinway grand piano. The show's young organiser later offered a spontaneous and sincere compliment.

'You'll be joining the staff soon,' he'd said.

His comment changed my life. It gave me the confidence to play in front of people again and master my nerves. So, I volunteered as a house pianist at three beautiful National Trust properties in Devon. I practised and then performed all my old classical pieces before crossing over to play jazz standards, pop ballads and love songs at a local bistro.

And then I landed a residency at a hotel in Babbacombe. I was well pleased.

I felt I was going up in the world.

Many guests at the hotel had come up to me and commented on how much they enjoyed my playing.

'Your phrasing is superb,' said one gentleman, who seemed to know something about music.

Such a lovely man - he's bound to have left a favourable comment on Trip Advisor about me, I thought.

'We really love your playing. We love how we can hear the melody so clearly,' said a very elegant lady as I exited the restaurant one evening. 'Some pianists play so many notes we have a job to pick out the tune,' she concluded.

Surely she will have left a good review about my playing?

I also received quite a few tips in money - fivers and even tenners now and again. On one occasion, while I was playing in a bistro, a man approached me and stuffed some money into the top of my music bag as I played. Out of the corner of my eye, I saw it was a £20 note, but at the end of the evening, when I put it in my purse, there were three £20 notes folded together. Crikey, sixty quid as a tip! That was more than my fee for the whole evening.

More often, someone would buy me a drink as an expression of their enjoyment of my artistry. I could only thank them for giving me the gift of listening.

Usually, people would simply applaud now and again to express their appreciation.

So with all that positive feedback, I was confident I'd see some lovely comments about the marvellous ambience I created during dinner in the restaurant.

I began at the top of the hotel reviews on Trip Advisor and worked backwards.

Nothing about the music.

Absolutely nothing.

I kept reading.

Bored with the lack of comments, I resorted to speed reading for the word "piano" or "pianist".

And there it was.

Someone mentioned a "piano player".

I read eagerly.

Then, I turned icy cold in shock.

2. THERE'S ALWAYS ONE...

Surely this was not ME and MY playing that was being described?

It was brutal.

But it had to be. Yes, when I looked at the date of the review.

And then I remembered the incident.

There was a special group in the hotel for their annual getaway amongst the other guests, who'd come into the restaurant for their evening meal towards the end of my gig.

I'd been playing my usual repertoire of love songs, pop ballads, and songs from the movies and shows during dinner to a very appreciative audience. The conversation volume in the dining room rose as this group took their seats to dine. To complement the now boisterous atmosphere, I played some swinging jazz standards, which created a more upbeat mood. I began with Gershwin and then segued to my Cole Porter set, starting with a song of his I'd recently learnt called "From This Moment On".

I'd been smitten by this piece when I'd heard Karen Carpenter sing it along to Richard Carpenter's arrangement using Bach's Prelude No. 2. The stunning fusion of Bach and Cole Porter made my jaw drop, giving me goosebumps on my goosebumps. I couldn't bring off Richard Carpenter's dazzling Bach arrangement, but my heart swelled with joy as I played the song, lost in the beauty of imagining Karen Carpenter singing the lush words in her deep, velvety contralto voice.

I was in mid-flow enjoying the cheeky, sexy semitones and jaunty rhythms when, from behind, a man shouted in my left ear, 'What's this piece called then?' as he peered over my shoulder at my sheet music.

He startled me, and my recently acquired muscle memory faltered momentarily as I hit a duff chord.

'It's a Cole Porter song called From This Moment On,' I rattled out quickly, as I played a wrong note while trying to play *and* talk at the same time.

'It's from the film Kiss Me Kate,' I explained at speed, striving to recover my muscle memory as yet another wrong note landed.

Now, I can multitask in the kitchen; I can multitask around the home; I can multitask in the garden. But I can't read music, play the piano *and* talk at the same time.

He disappeared, and I moved swiftly on to play some Andrew Lloyd Webber, which I knew well. But he came back now and again, hovering behind me. I could feel him there. I could see him out of the corner of my eye, looking over my shoulder at my music. He did this several times, and each time I saw him, an occasional wrong note would creep in as I anticipated that he'd come up and start asking me questions. He never spoke to me again, but it unsettled me and my playing for the final 20 minutes of my session.

I was disappointed in myself because, in addition to playing pianos that had seen better days—such as those with unresponsive actions, or playing too loudly, and a thousand and one other surprises a hotel piano could present—I had trained myself not to be distracted by *anything* when playing the piano.

Or at least, that's what I thought.

For a start, there's constant chatter and occasional loud laughter or giggling when playing in a dining room. During Christmas, random party poppers or blowers would sound off without warning.

Then right behind me in the restaurant was the loud clattering of plates as the waiting staff decided their dirty plate station was to be immediately behind the pianist. I don't know why, because the grand piano was elevated on a carpeted stage, along with a Liberace-style candlestick placed on the piano lid. The dirty plate station nearby spoiled the opulence.

I never realised how deafeningly loud crockery plates being stacked together could be. It always made me jump...oh, and then there was the odd fly that might buzz around and insist on landing on my sheet music, crawling up and down the pages, which was rather distracting.

Added to that, vagaries in temperature could be unpredictable - I'd be engulfed in heat with beads of sweat trickling down my forehead one minute, when suddenly out of nowhere, a chilling draught slithered its way from the kitchens behind me, swirling around my feet sending a shiver up my spine.

Then, while some evenings the restaurant food could smell quite appetising, if fish was on the menu, the odours that wafted around me could be a tad nauseating.

That's not to mention the whims of the guests. Now and again, there would be The Whistler - someone who would whistle along to every blummin' tune they could when they weren't eating. Then there was The Clapper - the guest who would clap after every piece. Whilst it was nice to have my playing praised with applause, when it happened all the time, it would cause me anxiety.

But my training to ignore anything and everything going on around me disappeared with this man's behaviour, which I found intimidating. But no one would know I'd made a few mistakes unless they knew the songs well.

But this man did know the songs well, as was clear in his review:

"There was an out-of-tune piano player, everyone else thought she was great, but we were laughing our socks off," wrote "mikey_man" from Bristol on Trip Advisor.

Ratbag!

I was tempted to send him a personal message on Trip Advisor with a link to my YouTube channel, where there wasn't a single wrong note to be heard. But I thought it best to ignore his comments. He'd been scathing about the hotel in general in his review; he was one of those grumpy guests who seemed to get pleasure from leaving negative comments.

...ouch! The chill of reading that review sent me into a state

of shock, and I had to have a cup of tea with a large tot of whisky in it.

Crikey…just goes to show, there's always one.

3. ONWARDS AND UPWARDS WITH SEAN CONNERY

'Oooh, you're gorgeous you are! You're absolutely GORGEOUS!'

Janine—one of the younger and more mobile residents of the care home for people with dementia—was dancing around me and my portable piano as I played "Que Sera Sera".

Surely she's not speaking to me?

Then, as she waltzed in front of my piano, I saw she was clutching one of the memory cards out in front of her, and as she twirled around, I glimpsed the handsome figure of Sean Connery as 007, gun and all.

I had to agree, he was rather gorgeous.

Then, so that I could keep Janine enjoying her waltz with Sean, I transitioned to playing "My Favourite Things" from *The Sound of Music*...oh but not before another resident, the placid Morag, with her sad, vacant eyes, came up to me with her usual question in her gentle, lilting Welsh brogue, 'Where should I go? What should I do?' *(Good questions!)*

'Sit down on that chair and they'll bring you a nice cup of tea and a biscuit,' was my stock answer which always seemed to reassure her.

Janine continued to waltz around me and my piano with Sean held in front of her, but then Dot decided to get up too as I continued *The Sound of Music* theme by playing "Edelweiss". The song triggered a response in her, and she came and stood in front of me. The care home I was playing at focused on people suffering mainly from dementia, and unlike other care homes where I played, many of the residents were physically mobile. Dot loved to come and stand in front of my portable piano and stroke my music as I played, telling me what a wonderful pianist I was.

'You're really good at playing the piano you are,' she'd coo as she gently ran her hands over the pages of my music, obscuring some of the music notes as she stroked them. Unfortunately, I cannot play by ear or from memory—I need the black dots—so I found this behaviour a little tricky. I sure was glad there was no "mikey_man" lurking in the care home as I navigated reading the music between Dot's fingers.

Contrary to popular belief, being a hotel pianist is not that well paid considering the level of skill required for the job. A self-employed plumber earns more per hour. Plus it's a very part-time job. I was playing for just three hours a week at the hotel: one and a half hours on a Wednesday night and one and a half hours on a Saturday night. So I'd looked for other work to augment my income and the opportunity arose through an agent to play in residential nursing and care homes once or twice a week. The pay was half what I earned as a hotel pianist (and I had to pay all my travel costs and cart all my heavy gear around with me for that) because the agent took the other half of the fee. But I was up for earning a bit of extra cash and I appreciated that the agent had to arrange all the appointments with the homes each month.

I always performed for the residents in care homes as if they were guests at the hotel. They weren't able to visit a nice hotel, but I could go to them and bring them the experience of music played in a posh restaurant.

However, at first, going into care homes was a shock, and there were aspects of the job I found difficult. On a few occasions, I left near to tears. The homes varied in atmosphere, smells and noises. Some were positively lovely, but a few were exceptionally grim. Thankfully, in most homes, it was life-enhancing for the residents to be there, and I found it very rewarding to work amongst these people on the last lap of their lives.

The shock of the Trip Advisor review lingered in my mind for a long time, but I knew it was a one-off for me. Besides, even concert pianists make the odd mistake now and again. I tried to convince myself that even great pianists like Rubinstein and Lang Lang might have played a wrong note if someone had crept up behind them and shouted in their left ear, 'What's this piece called then?' So I carried on enjoying the job, though perhaps there should have been a sign over the piano: "Please don't shoot the pianist. She is doing her best." (Thank you, Oscar Wilde, for that idea).

I was glad that "mikey_man" wasn't local to Torbay, and his group only visited the hotel once a year for their annual getaway. I noted in my diary when their next visit to the hotel was due, though I never saw them again. And the hotel management never said a word to me about the bad review. They must have read it, but I carried on playing there until the hotel closed down a few years later. The hotel itself also had its fair share of bad reviews, and they knew how difficult some clients could be.

After the hotel closed, I got a few bookings at an up-market hotel in East Devon through an agent. It had a large communal lounge at the front with open sea views leading to a small, intimate bar at the back, where a beautiful Blüthner grand piano graced the room. Some of the guests enjoyed their canapés and a glass of champers before dinner in this cosy space, where sofas were smattered with beautiful scatter cushions.

It was just the sort of venue I loved to play at. *Gosh, I shall enjoy playing here,* I thought as I set up my music, *what a beautiful place.*

I began playing some soft jazz, including a superb arrangement of "Killing Me Softly", where the gentle, sexy chords enhanced the sumptuous melody and transported me to another world.

BANG! CRASH!

The barman threw several empties into a bin behind the bar, making me jump. *Blummin' heck!*

What a shock! I wasn't expecting that.

Recovering my composure, I played on.

RATTLE, RATTLE, RATTLE, RATTLE went the ice cubes in his cocktail shaker. I can tell you now, that making a cocktail is a VERY noisy business. The rattling went on and on while he mixed several cocktails.

BANG! CRASH! Went more empties as they landed in the bin.

Cripes! What a racket!

I played on, regardless, yet disappointed that the soothing ambience I was creating with my music had been rudely interrupted.

SSSSSSSSHHHHHHHHHHHHHHHHHhhhhhhh…

Gordon Bennett! Next, it was the deafening sound of loud steam from the coffee machine milk frother, which went on and on and on as the barman produced several cappuccinos.

Crikey, for a small bar, it sure is noisy!

I played on.

SWISH SWOOSH, SWISH SWOOSH…

Well, knock me down with a feather, I don't believe it! By way of an encore from the barman, there came the swish-swooshing of a noisy dishwasher from behind the bar just as I began a soft version of "Close To You".

RATTLE, RATTLE, RATTLE, RATTLE.

BANG! CRASH!

It was the same every week. Noise, noise, noise.

Added to that, I was often frozen stiff from the air conditioning, which was immediately above the piano. Despite wrapping my coat around my legs, my feet were like blocks of ice.

I confess I was quite relieved when the owner of the bar sold up, including the piano. It wasn't one of my favourite venues in the end.

What a disappointment.

I was fortunate to find another residency as a pianist in a newly refurbished hotel in Torquay soon after. Ever on the vigil for any mikey_type_men, I scoured the Trip Advisor reviews of this new hotel after I'd been playing there a few months, and thankfully, it was all good - not only for the entertainment but also for the hotel, which was excellent in every way.

But I learnt that Trip Advisor could be a two-edged sword and a scourge for any establishment, no matter how amazing it is. It wasn't just me who'd had an unpleasant experience - there's always that grumpy client who doesn't like some silly thing and will leave a bad review to get revenge. This new hotel had fallen victim to such a reviewer, only this time the feisty hotel owner had responded in no uncertain terms, informing the Trip Adviser readers that this client had deliberately lied and that when he'd been politely challenged in the restaurant about his obstreperous behaviour, he'd made a scene by dropping his trousers.

Hmmm. Yes, there's always one…

4. FISH PASTE SANDWICHES

"Viking, North Utsire, South Utsire, southerly or south-westerly four or five occasionally six at first…"

My car radio relayed the British Shipping Forecast.

"Forties, Cromarty, Forth, Tyne, Dogger, south or southwest, four or five decreasing three at times, showers, thundery at times…"

It was 5.55 p.m. on Sunday, 3rd September 2020, and I was driving to work to play the piano during dinner for the first time in nearly six months following the lockdown.

For four years, I had listened to the Shipping Forecast on Sunday evenings as I travelled to the hotel. But the Coronavirus had forced all restaurants and hotels to shut down, and musicians like myself were bottom of the pile in returning to work. We were considered to be a health concern by the government, and although hotels had opened in July, entertainers had to wait another two months before we could resume our roles.

I hadn't realised how much I had missed this rhythmic radio transmission: the transmission of a virus had cut my routine.

Hearing the Shipping Forecast again was like balm.

Poetic.

Calming.

Evocative.

Strange-sounding names that I never quite understood. But I loved them. Their effect on me was stronger than any piece of music just then. Hearing the British Shipping Forecast was like pressing the Reset button. Its hypnotic rhythms truncated my life into one whole, time-travelling. It was like a thread, linking pre-COVID to post-COVID: a secret tunnel from past to present, soothing and hopeful.

Constant.

Almost eternal.

"...Dover, Wight, Portland, Plymouth..."

It evoked the aura of my childhood, of summer Sunday sabbaths over half a century ago: a different kind of lockdown then, when the shops were shut for different reasons.

"...Biscay variable three or less, rain for a time, mainly good..." cooed the soothing voice on Radio 4.

A flashback to lonely Sunday evenings for me and my father while my mother was out working at the Royal Orthopaedic Hospital in Birmingham as a domestic cleaner. The winsome tinkling of an ice cream van would sound a few streets away, and the smell of fish paste in the sandwiches my mother had left me for tea mingled with the smoke from my father's cigarette. He only ever smoked at weekends.

As the memories surfaced, work beckoned as I drove to the hotel. Tonight, I was to be a merrymaker for a coach load of people while they enjoyed a six-course dinner—a very different Sunday evening from those decades ago as a lonely child—yet both eras glued together by the unchanging words...

"...Irish Sea, southwest veering northwest five to seven, showers, good. Shannon, southwest veering northwest five to seven, showers good. Rockall, northwest five to seven...Faeroes, southeast Iceland..."

The sequins on my evening dress felt uncomfortable as they dug in under my arms.

Then came the Big Ben gongs on the radio ringing out for the Six O'Clock news. My mind slipped back in time, back to those fish paste sandwiches, back to the 1960s, back to Birmingham where I'd grown up.

It seemed like another planet back then, and a yearning for something of that era surfaced, even though in many ways life wasn't any better back then. But I couldn't deny it: there was a simplicity and sweetness about life in the 60s which seemed to have evaporated, and for several days, the longing for those times lingered in my mind as memories came flooding back.

It is difficult to convey the feeling of a 1960s childhood

to younger generations. How is it possible to communicate another time, another place? The sights, the sounds, the smells? An estranged era, gone forever? How do I process it for myself even? I'd never really thought about it before - the past was the past and forgotten about, with focus and energies on the present and the future.

Often, it is the smallest, most insignificant of memories that come to mind, and to record these in such detail is not to everyone's taste, but a memoir is a memoir, and many authors include the smallest of observations to convey a personal story. It is up to the reader whether they gloss over such details or decide to absorb the information.

Growing up in the 60s felt like inhabiting two worlds. One part of you was drawn back into the remnants of Victoriana—experiencing the last vestiges of Victorian life—while another part of you was propelled into a modern future, poised on the brink of a new era, characterised by emerging technologies, new methods of governance, and different social behaviours.

But it was the scraps from the past which lingered most in my memory. In that sense, I am privileged to have experienced the last pickings of an age which has now gone forever, and the words of Flora Thompson come to mind when she wrote in *Lark Rise to Candleford* about her 19th-century childhood, "This last picking, though meagre, was sweet."

So here are a few of my last pickings from a time and place now no longer in existence...

5. QUE SERA SERA BABY BOOMER

My father's heart was in his boots.

It was the 4th of June 1959, and he'd just been to Marston Green Maternity Hospital to see me—his newborn daughter—through the glass of the nursery while the midwife held me up for inspection (husbands were not allowed to be present at the birth of their babies back then).

But it was the sight of me, wrinkled and red, that shook him to the core. In that moment, I resembled an alien creature, a tiny being from a distant galaxy. The disappointment on his face was palpable, a mix of surprise and sadness.

Unable to bear the weight of his emotions, after a cursory nod to the midwife, he swiftly turned away, his footsteps echoing down the hospital corridor.

The world outside was alive with the vibrant colours of summer, the sun casting a warm golden glow, at odds with his grim feelings.

Seeking solace, he made his way to The Three Horseshoes pub in Sheldon, where his older sister, Ann, presided over the bustling establishment.

He needed a stiff drink.

'What's up with you?' were the first words out of Ann's mouth as my father went up to the bar, his face betraying his disappointment.

'I've just been to see Dawn at the hospital, and she's ugly!' he blurted out, holding back the tears.

'Don't be silly, Les! All newborn babies are ugly. She'll change as she grows, you mark my words. Here, have a whisky, looks like you need it.'

Me, about 11 months old in 1960

My father, Les, was born in 1931 and was one of the youngest of thirteen children, or (to use his own words) he was "bottom of the pile." They were a poor family, and being "bottom of the pile" meant he had to sit on wooden orange crates to eat dinner as there weren't enough chairs to go around the table. He lived at 41 Cherrywood Road, Bordesley Green, with his parents, Rosina and Arthur Smith, along with several siblings who were still living at home - though the older ones had flown the nest. There were actually fifteen children, but two had died in infancy.

Quite how my paternal ancestors came to settle in Birmingham is unclear, but like many during the Industrial Revolution, it was likely to do with finding work.

On census records and birth certificates that I have, my paternal grandparents and great-grandparents are recorded as having curious occupations such as tube drawer, Britannia metal burnisher, hair curlers press worker, iron ore worker, bone button maker, smith's stoker and plumber's zinc worker, as well as more familiar employment such as cab driver (which would have been horse and cart), coach builder, brass worker and French polisher.

The interwar years (1918-1939) were a pivotal period in the evolution of social welfare in the United Kingdom. The impact of poverty during this time prompted significant reforms that ultimately led to the dismantling of the outdated Poor Law system. The abolition of workhouses, the disappearance of the Poor Law Guardians, the elimination of the "workhouse test," and the rejection of the terms "pauper" and "pauperism" all marked important steps towards a more humane and effective approach to poverty relief.

Nevertheless, the dread and horror of the workhouse were likely never far from their minds, and many of them—both male and female—went from one job to another to avoid unemployment and the poverty it could lead to.

If only some of them had written memoirs!

Like most of his generation, my father was traumatised by the effects of the Second World War as a child. Not long before he died, he told me how, as a boy, he was terrified of the German planes which flew over the skies of industrial Birmingham, dropping bombs. He said it stoked up a wave of intense anger in him. As he and his family all crowded in the Anderson shelter, holed up in the earth and corrugated metal, he'd hold up his fist as the dull drone of the bomber planes sounded overhead, and feeling disempowered, he'd shout at the bombers to fuck off.

He was convinced he was going to die.

To experience the terror of death at such a young age was damaging.

My father's mother, Rosina, was a devout Catholic and sent all her children to Catholic school. His keenest memory of his school days was that the nuns only ever gave him the triangle to play during music lessons, but he so wanted to play the big bass drum.

He left school at the age of fourteen.

To get some decent clobber and a good pair of shoes that didn't leak, he applied to join the Royal Navy. He passed the entrance examination with some help from his brother-in-law, but he was rejected twice because he was too underweight. The doctor undertaking the medical had lifted my father's thin, puny arm and shook his head, 'You need a bit more meat on you, lad,' he'd said.

My father was thrilled when he was finally accepted as an Able Seaman and joined the Royal Navy on 12 October 1948, at the age of 18. He wanted to see the world.

My mother, Barbara, was born in 1935 and was proudly one of the "Jubilee babies". If she were alive today, I just know she would have been made up that the Coronation of King Charles III took place on her birthday - 6th May.

She lived at 103 Birdbrook Road, Great Barr, with her parents, Doris and Tom Davies, along with three sisters and a younger brother —a much smaller family than my father's.

Tom was Welsh from Porthcawl. Not much is known about why he moved to Birmingham, though it was very likely to do with finding work as a motor mechanic. When his son, Roy, was born, he famously remarked, 'Thank God there's another pair of balls in the house'.

My mother always liked to look smart and well-dressed, and even though money was tight, her clothes and shoes were always stylish. She occasionally boasted over the years that on her school leaving certificate, the Headteacher had written that she was "always clean and tidy."

My mother, Barbara, circa 1953

Of my maternal grandparents' background, I know very little. Neither of them disclosed much about their past. But one thing I do know about Tom is that he was a potshot at killing flies. He did this by rolling a small piece of newspaper into a tiny ball and then catapulting the missile with an elastic band at any fly that happened to have landed in the living room. My mother was in awe of her father's aim and precision and told me this story several times over the years. I never got to witness this amazing ability of his as he passed away before I got to know him, but it was a memory my mother cherished.

After Tom had died, a story often told with fondness was how he could get creative where his family's recreation was concerned - even though it entailed a somewhat unorthodox approach.

During sunny summer weekends, Tom would sometimes price up a car for repair and tell the client it would be ready in two days. But then, after they'd left, he would say, 'Doris! Get the kids ready! I'll have that car fixed in two hours, let's take them to the seaside for the day.'

Then great excitement would ensue as they packed a picnic and revelled in a glorious car ride to the coast, making cherished memories together, luxuriating in the freedom of such leisure and pleasure, their laughter filling the air.

Tom wasn't able to afford holidays or a car himself, and his motive for "borrowing" one was fuelled by a desire to ensure his family didn't miss out, and for that, I do not judge him.

Both my parents were traumatised by the Second World War, and for my mother, this manifested itself in toilet anxiety. She was quite open about it, and if she was out anywhere, she rarely passed a loo without going in for a "tinkle" (this was her euphemism for doing a pee due to the tinkling sound it made as it hit the water in the pan). She told us this issue went back to her childhood when she was evacuated to Wales during the war. She and her two sisters, Brenda and Ruth, boarded the train in Birmingham, waved goodbye to their mother, not knowing if they'd ever see her again, and off they went with their gas masks in tow. They all wet themselves with fear on the train. This traumatising event stayed with her for life.

On the subject of my birth, I was nearly never born. Twice. Well, possibly three times...though come to think of it, I was nearly never born four times if I count Harry.

Harry was my mother's first boyfriend, but she ditched him after he sang to her the 1920's Broadway song, "I'm just wild about Harry, and Harry's wild about me!" in a pub in front of all their buddies. This presumptuous, flirtatious behaviour disgusted her. She was not wild about him at all.

But what if she had been? Well then, I wouldn't be here to tell the tale.

Next, I was nearly never born when my teenage mother was dating a rather trendy young man, and he had a burning question for her.

'Are you a virgin?' he asked, bold as brass, as they rode in the back seat of his friend's posh open-top car.

'No, I'm Church of England,' was my mother's serious and innocent reply (I kid you not).

This story was told to me several times over the years by my mother with, I might say, a degree of embarrassment that she'd been so naive and ignorant about his question. She'd thought the word "virgin" had to do with the Virgin Mary and Catholicism.

She never saw that young man again but met my rather handsome father instead.

My father, Les, circa 1952

However, I most definitely would not have entered this world had it not been for the First World War.

This is because my paternal grandmother, Rosina, would never have married my grandfather had it not been for the fact that her first husband, Henry Jarvis, was killed in action (KIA) on the Somme in July 1916, leaving her with three young children.

What was she to do?

With no social security or benefits, she had little choice but to find another husband, though with so many men away fighting the war, there weren't many left at home.

Enter, then, my grandfather—Arthur Smith—into her young life. Arthur's real name was George Jolley, though we never found out why he changed his name. It is shrouded in mystery. He was four years younger than my grandmother, and on my father's birth certificate, his occupation is "General labourer".

Arthur had a slight stammer, and also an impediment in his feet and was not fit for military service. He joined the King's Royal Rifle Corps as a Private (1307) on 25th August 1914 at Winchester under his real name, George Jolley, but he was discharged a month later as being "medically unfit".

How and when Arthur and Rosina met is unknown, but they married on 22nd November 1917, and she went on to have ten more children with Arthur. He was a brass worker and general labourer, though despite many of his generation being illiterate, he had learned to read and write and was good with numbers.

My father told me that Arthur had beautiful copperplate handwriting. In addition to this, all the local men used to flock to him so that he could work out their winnings from the betting office - no doubt aided and abetted by the fact that his brother-in-law, Jack Bottrill (who'd married Arthur's sister, Lucy), was a bookmaker. Back then, if someone bet on a winning horse, the bookies would ask the punter how much they had coming back to them, knowing that many of the men weren't able to tot up their winnings. So Arthur was in much demand - no doubt being paid in ciggies or a bit of commission. My father called Arthur a "loveable rogue", though quite what he meant by that wasn't exactly clear.

One of my aunts recalled that Arthur was always impeccably dressed, often sporting a crisp, white muffler (a type of neck garment) and highly polished shoes - even though the soles had gone and were lined with cardboard, as many of the family's shoes were. Despite the hardship, being well-dressed was a common attribute for many working-class people in the 20th century, along with a high standard of cleanliness and personal hygiene. Poverty didn't prevent pride in their appearance, making the effort to be well turned out.

They were a poor family, and life was hard. But my grandmother was a woman of great resolve, resilience, and resourcefulness. To give her children fruit, she would ask the seller for bruised ones, which were given without charge. She would then skillfully remove the damage with a knife, giving each child a piece of fresh fruit in turn.

Arthur died in 1956, and as the family began to leave home, my grandmother worked in a laundry, and at one point in a bar where she told my father about a Jewish customer who would regularly ask for a "beef pie" with his pint, knowing full well it was really a "pork pie". Calling it a different name was helpful!

One of my grandmother's few luxuries in life was to enjoy a "sticky pint" - a stout beer from a local outdoor (a shop that sold draught beer) where the amount was measured with a stick - hence the name "sticky pint". On warm summer evenings, these sticky pints would be relished by the women sitting on their front doorsteps, enjoying a neighbourly natter. Although they were testing times, the sense of community was strong with a common bond born from poverty.

At some point in the late 50s, my grandmother moved and settled in 55 Cherrywood Road, a small two-bedroomed house with a shared outside toilet between several other houses. The presence of Prince, her vigilant Alsatian, added a feeling of security to the surroundings. The atmosphere inside was filled with the earthy whiff of coal from the coal hole under the stairs. The kitchen, a small area at the foot of the staircase, had a sink with a cold water tap, a gas cooker and a free-standing cupboard. When she did the dishes - no draining board - she washed an item, dried it and put it in the cupboard. A stark contrast to the sleek, modern kitchens her grandchildren enjoy today.

The First World War may have ended in 1918 but for my grandmother—and many women like her—the battle had only just begun in many ways, with a life of hardship ahead for them. She died in January 1963 when I was three, so I never knew her, but I sense she had an inner vitality as she raised her large family at a time in history when life was challenging for all classes of people, whether rich or poor.

I owe my existence to the horror of the First World War and the remarriage of my grandmother to Arthur. A sobering thought.

I was nearly never born a fourth time when my mother called off her engagement to my father in 1954. This fact is routinely recorded by my father in his 1954 naval diary, where he records on Wednesday 15th September 1954 ~

"I received a letter from Barbara, she packed me up."

Quite what caused my mother to pack him up is unclear, though there are clues in my father's diary including his entry a few months earlier on 6th May 1954 ~

"Barbara's birthday today and I haven't even sent her a card, I bet she is fed up!!"

However, during his travels around "the Med" that year as an Able Seaman (Gunnery) on board HMS Warrior, he bought my mother several gifts: some underwear, a blouse, a set of pearls, a Kimono and a music box. Throughout his life, the giving of gifts was my father's primary "love language", and I often wonder whether these gifts won my mother back over to him, for they were married in 1955.

Courting days

My mother on her wedding day.
They married in Birmingham Registry Office.

My father was still in the Royal Navy, stationed at Devonport, and after they married they moved to Plymouth, lodging in digs at 77 Alexander Road. My mother loved Plymouth and she was particularly fond of her landlords, Mr & Mrs Reed, keeping in touch with them for many years. She had a lifelong desire to return to Plymouth - sadly only realised upon her death as she requested that her ashes be scattered into the sea near Plymouth Hoe.

When my father left the Royal Navy on 7 March 1956, they moved back to Birmingham and lived in a council flat at 1/99 Prescott Street, in Hockley, B18. My father got a job on the track at Land Rover in Solihull (where he worked until he retired), and my mother found a job at H. Samuel Jewellers, being very happy working there in the shop.

...And so, despite some near misses, I was born on the 4th of June 1959, the firstborn to my parents.

Another daughter, Diane, was stillborn in 1962 (sadly due to complications of Toxeamia), and my sister Elizabeth was born in 1967.

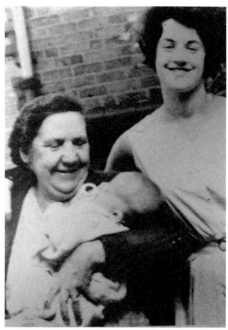

My mother, and me being held by my paternal grandmother, Rosina - 1959.

Early in 1962, my parents moved from their flat in Hockley to a three-bedroom council house on Wasdale Road, Northfield, in the then leafy county of Worcestershire (now in the West Midlands). And that's where I grew up, and my earliest memories begin...

6. WASDALE ROAD

'I...scream! I...scream!' bellowed the minuscule man, his voice reverberating through the air, leaving us in awe of its unexpected power.

One of my earliest recollections of Wasdale Road involves the ice cream man, as he pushed his white square-box barrow along our street screaming, "I...scream," selling his ice cream. Eagerly, I would dash outside to purchase a tub of velvety vanilla for a few pennies.

Another memory etched in my mind is that of the rag-and-bone man, along with his trusty horse and cart ambling along. His cries of "any old iron, any old iron!" echoed through the neighbourhood. A relic of the Victorian era, he seemed out of place, yet undeniably present. If the horse blessed the ground with its droppings, the first fortunate neighbour would swiftly scoop up the manure to nourish their thriving garden veggies.

These memories—juxtaposing the booming voice of the tiny man and the rag-and-bone man—paint a vivid picture of life on working-class Wasdale Road.

In her book *Lark Rise to Candleford*, Flora Thompson vividly portrays "poor people's houses" in rural Oxfordshire during the 1880s as "brick boxes with blue-slated roofs", and this description perfectly depicts many of the council houses in Birmingham during the 60s.

They were built post-war, and these dwellings—often boasting three bedrooms—were constructed with sturdy bricks and featured blue-slated roofs. They all had their own bathroom and toilet indoors. Gone were the days of back-to-back houses when several families shared an outside latrine.

Wasdale Road was a serene street adorned with sticky sycamore trees, situated on the southern side of the city in the leafy suburb of Northfield. The street seamlessly connected to the end of the more upmarket Lockwood Road, which was lined from top to bottom with privately owned semi-detached houses - a big step above our rented council properties.

We lived at number 25, an end-of-terrace dwelling opposite a tranquil cul-de-sac called Westcliffe Place. The bottom of Wasdale Road gently sloped into Colworth Road - a slope I loved because I'd freewheel my tricycle down it, coming to a halt by bumping into the large tree at the bottom.

What I adored most about our house was the small window at the top of the landing, which flooded the hall with warm, natural light on sunny days. My utmost delight, however, came from us having an entryway on the side with a back gate—a perk from being an end-of-terrace house—expanding our garden's breadth. The dustbin was kept at the end of the entry, and each week, the bin man would let himself into our garden to empty it, carrying it on his shoulders up the garden path.

There was a raised border down the entry, where several mature peony plants grew. In summer, they blossomed, oozing blood-red flowers as big as saucers, their giant blooms forever a backdrop in my childhood memory.

Another early memory is of my father on summer Sunday mornings, meticulously trimming the privet hedge with his shears, their snip-snip, snip-snip-snip echoing through the air. Then afterwards, the beautiful rhythmic dance of the lawnmower would commence as he pushed it back and forth, its gentle swish-whoosh, swish-whoosh, being a memorable sound of mechanical precision, mystery and mastery, now gone forever.

The front garden flourished with vibrant flowers popular in the 1960s, such as London pride, sweet William, and fragrant pinks. The pinks were my favourite - their intoxicating scent tempting a child's nose to take a deep sniff, while snapdragons, with their bulbous blooms, captivated a child's eyes as bees buzzed in and out of the colourful flowers.

The "brick box" council houses, compact and cosy, featured a three-up, three-down layout. Each had net curtains for privacy - though my mother opted for plain pale lemon nets with frills along the bottom, crisscrossing in the middle and pulled back with frilly ties.

A living room at the front looked onto the street, while a kitchen and tiny bathroom were at the back. Connected to the kitchen were a small pantry and a coal house. The floor covering in the bathroom and kitchen was lino, where the ends curled up at the extremities.

I loved the pantry. Amongst other things, there often lurked a bowl of vinegary stewed salad of onion, cucumber and tomatoes—all gone soft in the vinegar—a zingy, savoury concoction tingling the tastebuds.

The whitewashed walls of the pantry glimmered, reflecting the gentle rays of sunlight that filtered through a tiny window. Freezing in winter and cool in summer, the pantry kept our food fresh as we had no fridge in the early 60s.

Ascending the stairs from the front door, a small landing led to three bedrooms: a larger bedroom at the front with two smaller bedrooms at the back.

Space in the house was limited, but essentials were present - a sideboard, a drop-leaf dining table with four chairs, a small three-piece suite, a television, and a petite coffee table filled the snug lounge.

The bedrooms, although compact, were furnished with a bed, a wardrobe, and a dressing table.

Yet these "brick boxes" were sheer luxury compared to what previous generations of poor people in Birmingham and other parts of Britain dwelt in, many of them surviving in the overcrowded "back-to-back" houses with only one toilet between four dwellings.

The 1960s brought a rise in the standard of living for the

working classes, enabling them to have a little more disposable income for saving or spending.

This increase in wealth, it seems, was because of pressure from the unions. Strikes, fuelled by the unions, were commonplace, and I often accompanied my father to sign on at the "Labour Exchange" (the brainchild of Sir Winston Churchill) to collect his dues when he was off work because he was on strike. But maybe there were other economic factors as to why the working classes enjoyed better living standards during the 1960s, including perhaps being the beneficiaries of capitalism - who knows?

My father was an avid supporter of the Labour Party for many years. I sometimes accompanied him when he canvassed for them, posting flyers through people's doors in the run-up to General Elections. He maintained the belief that the Labour Party was on his side and had improved his standard of living over the years—he never forgot the poverty of his childhood.

But times changed, and my father became politically homeless when he lost all connection with the Labour Party under Tony Blair. He just couldn't get the drift of "New Labour" values at all. What he wanted was "true Labour"—a party that was on the side of working people and the underdog, so he very reluctantly defected to UKIP (UK Independence Party) as a last resort. There was no way he could ever vote "Tory" (as he called the Conservatives), and he felt disconnected from the Liberal Democrats, but his vote lacked the conviction he had once held in the socialism that had lifted him out of the poverty of his youth.

During the early 60s, we had a coal fire in the living room, but the rest of the house was unheated. The bitter chill of winter seeped through the cracks, causing shivers to run down our spines.

"Shut that door!" was a phrase made famous by comedian

Larry Grayson, but it truly was a familiar saying in our home by my father during the winter months. Mind you, when he said it, he'd revert to an old form of Birmingham dialect, and it came out as "Shut that doe-er!" It seemed that pronouncing "door" as "doe-er" emphasised his annoyance when one of us would fail to keep the draughts out.

In the larger front bedroom where my parents slept, there was a tiny coal fire installed in the wall, but I never saw my mother ever light it. It was too much trouble.

She kept a potty under the bed - and quite right too as it was a long way down the stairs in the dead of night for a pee and freezing in the winter.

In my bedroom at the back, there was an airing cupboard situated underneath an "immersion heater" which my mother put on once a week so we could all take a bath. If it was left on for too long, it would boil away noisily, rumbling like thunder. But gone were the days when poor people bathed in each other's water in a tin bath in front of the fire.

The weekly visit from the coal man, along with his horse and cart, was an event I enjoyed. The thunderous noise of the coals being tipped into the coal house reverberated throughout the house, creating an exciting sound effect.

But the government's Clean Air Act of 1956 meant more and more council homes were fitted with gas fires, and by the mid-60s, the weekly visit of the coal man became a thing of the past.

This new source of heating was met with total approval from my mother.

'We don't want any more of those pea-soupers and smogs. They killed people. And no more cleaning the grate for me,' was her verdict on gas fires.

She also preferred gas as she believed it to be safer than open fires, especially for children who were vulnerable to getting too close to a fire and their clothes catching alight, resulting in life-changing injuries. There were no fire-retardant clothes in those days.

So we, along with everyone else in Wasdale Road, made the change from coal to gas. My parents had the original tiled grate removed and replaced it with a modern teak "surround" that encompassed the gas fire, upon which were placed many different kinds of brass ornaments. My mother loved it.

But we kept our old coal fire tool kit, which stood on the "surround" for many years, just for show. There was a shovel, a pair of tongs and a round brush with black bristles. It was my favourite ornament.

During the 60s, my parents redecorated our home from top to bottom. My mother insisted on the best anaglypta wallpaper for the lounge, though we had cheap woodchip wallpaper in the bedrooms.

In a drastic bid to eradicate the dated look of our lounge, my parents had the old 1940s solid wooden doors removed and replaced with glass doors. They were a huge improvement, and the glass had an elegant fern leaf pattern woven into it, giving our living room a truly modern feel.

My parents were delighted to have the means to purchase a plush new carpet to adorn our living room, which my mother meticulously selected. She was adamant that it must be an Axminster carpet. She had good taste when it came to textiles and fabrics. It was a luxurious woollen masterpiece that exuded a velvety softness underfoot. The gentle *swish swoosh* of her beloved Ewbank carpet sweeper gliding over the pile of the sumptuous floor covering was a familiar sound.

The carpet was my mother's pride and joy, and she chose Axminster's colourful brand-new design based on a gas flame. It was bang on trend, matching the new gas fires being installed. The carpet's fibres, intricately woven, whispered against our soles as we traversed the room, while the vibrant hues of the pattern painted a vivid picture before our eyes of warmth and comfort.

Our Axminster carpet design - "High Speed Gas"
from The 1968 Designs from Axminster Carpets Ltd.
Used by permission.
(As an aside, when Axminster Carpets kindly sent through this image, the name
of the design was "Brixham" - the town I moved to when I married in 1994. My
mother would have considered that to have been a cosmic coincidence I'm sure!)

Not only that, my mother was determined to have the very best underlay for the carpet. She told me it would be so thick, soft and bouncy it would be like a trampoline.

As soon as the carpet was laid, I eagerly tested out the trampoline-like qualities of this luxury underlay. I leapt up high, planning to land on my knees, then bounce back up and land back on my feet. But the sound of my knees hitting the ground with a thud echoed in the room.

Ouch!

The impact sent a sharp pain shooting through my body.

The underlay was far from the trampoline my mother had described.

What a disappointment.

My mother had watched me do it before she could stop me

and hadn't anticipated that I would put her hyperbole figure of speech to the test. She was caught off guard, and I don't think she knew whether to laugh or cry. I could smell the familiar scent of her face cream as she gave me a warm hug, her hand gently rubbing my sore knees. Looking back, it was quite funny how I had taken my mother's words so literally. What a strange child I was.

Accompanying this opulent addition, a new three-piece suite graced our living space, emanating a gentle *creak* as we settled into its comforting embrace. The air in the room carried a hint of newness, a subtle aroma of fresh upholstery—albeit green PVC with soft brown nylon cushions—that mingled with the scent of polished wood, inviting us to relax and unwind. My mother loved her pouffe. 'I'm going to put my feet up and have a cup of tea,' was a daily mantra and routine for her.

Then, towards the end of the decade, we embarked on a trend that swept through our neighbourhood - that of integrating our pantry and coal house with the kitchen to make it bigger.

The sound of hammers striking against walls, along with the mingling smells of sawdust and paint wafting through the house, was a heady blend that spoke of transformation and progress.

We revelled in the modernity of our new kitchen, and with the pantry gone, my parents purchased a small refrigerator that had a tiny freezer compartment to make ice cubes - luxury!

But amidst all these upgrades, it was the Axminster carpet that truly captured my mother's heart. Its fiery design, inspired by the dance of gas flames, brought a warmth that transcended the physical realm.

With each step, the carpet whispered stories of comfort and elegance, embracing us in a tactile symphony of cosiness.

In the realm of our living room, sights, sounds, smells, and feelings intertwined, creating a sensory tapestry that mirrored the essence of the 60s and the love my mother poured into her cherished space.

My father proudly rented a black and white television from Radio Rentals, its flickering screen casting a dim glow in the room with our favourite 60s programs. I could almost smell the faint whiff of dust lingering on the old television set, full of static.

Oddly, in the early 90s, I too rented a TV from Radio Rentals sharing my father's false belief that renting a TV was cheaper than buying one - a notion that seemed to defy logic, for we never once encountered any technical glitches with our trusty rented televisions.

Meanwhile, the working-class neighbourhood buzzed with the arrival of telephones.

But not in our home.

My father resisted this latest device, and if we needed to make a telephone call, it was a long trek up Lockwood Road to the smelly, draughty phone boxes outside the Post Office on Bristol Road. It wasn't until the mid-80s that my father finally decided to embrace the convenience of a telephone.

Cars were another novelty just creeping into the lives of working-class people, but again my father resisted, and neither he nor my mother ever learned to drive. They had no desire to own or drive a car, and both preferred to travel by public transport.

Outside in our backyard, a neglected mangle stood silently, a relic from the past. Quite where my parents got it from remains a mystery - they had obviously brought it with them from their previous home in Hockley. I never saw my mother use it once, preferring a small electric spin dryer in the kitchen.

The yard gave way to a vibrant flower bed bursting with colour, releasing a gentle floral scent into the air, melting into a long lawn, its emerald green blades tickling any bare feet that dared to traverse it.

Alongside the lawn, a narrow path paved with grey weathered slabs guided one's steps, while a lengthy washing line swung rhythmically overhead on windy days. The long wooden "prop" that held up the line—often full of weighty washing drying in the breeze—stood tall, its rough surface capable of inflicting painful splinters upon unsuspecting hands.

On the other side of the path to the right was a long vegetable patch, difficult to keep free of weeds, so my parents decided to splash out and have it "turfed". But first, a rotten old shed, suspected of containing asbestos, had to be got rid of, and my father decided to deconstruct this item himself, resulting in his face blowing up like a balloon one morning (my mother reckoned it was a reaction to either the asbestos or the rats which the shed had been home to).

The wonderful thing about our terrace of five houses was that they boasted exceptionally long back gardens, each showcasing a magnificent expanse of greenery, shrubs, roses and flowers separated by unsightly grey wooden palings, adding an element of contrast to the scene.

Towards the end of the decade, my father diligently saved enough money to invest in a new cedar wood shed and a greenhouse, which were duly erected at the bottom of the garden. The sight of vibrant tomatoes and marrows thriving in the greenhouse brought a burst of colour to the surroundings. Nearby, a marvellous rubbish dump—one of my favourite places —emitted a faint odour, mingling with the pungent aroma of a giant horseradish plant and the earthy scent of my father's runner beans.

Added to the enchantment of our garden, a fabulous new swing stood proudly on the lush lawn. Its sleek green metal frame and wooden seat invited me to spend countless hours swaying back and forth. The rhythmic creaking of the swing blended harmoniously with the chirping of birds and the rustling of leaves in the breeze. With each ascent, the velocity created a thrilling sensation against my skin. I'd pull hard on the swing to increase the height. As I reached the pinnacle of each swing, a feeling of weightlessness consumed me, and I'd often leap off into the open air, landing in a heap.

But those few seconds after leaving the seat of the swing—weightless and airborne—were sensational.

Then, in the early 70s, a further glimmer of prosperity graced our lives once again as my father managed to save enough money to pay for a small "conservatory" to be built on the back of the kitchen. My mother insisted on calling it a "conservatory" (not a "verandah"), and my father insisted on paying cash for it, as he detested any kind of debt. Acquiring anything "on the knock" was not his thing at all, though my mother would occasionally buy a garment for herself from Mrs Mac's Grattan catalogue, paying off a little each week from her earnings as a hospital domestic.

The rich, fresh aroma of cedar wood from the conservatory permeated the garden, mingling with the earthy scent of the freshly creosoted beams. The sight of the meticulously built structure brought a sense of pride and accomplishment to my father.

At the back of our garden was a lush playing field stretching out, and many an hour was spent there after school playing under the giant oak tree that graced the grounds.

Then, over to the right at the bottom of our garden was a vast area of land full of allotments where many residents on the surrounding estates grew vegetables. A kaleidoscope of butterflies danced their way into our gardens, their delicate wings fluttering gracefully, bringing a touch of enchantment to our surroundings.

And so it was that living on Wasdale Road gifted a unique and distinct experience, full of 60s character. It exuded a distinct charm born from the remnants of the post-war era, the nostalgic memories of childhood, and the ever-changing dynamics that adorned our little corner of the world.

7. NEIGHBOURS, EVERYBODY NEEDS GOOD NEIGHBOURS...

A large part of the charm and character of Wasdale Road were the neighbours who lived closest to us. They were a mix of people; my parents were of the younger generation.

It has to be said that despite being a close-knit neighbourhood, everyone respected each other's personal space and social interactions tended to happen mainly over the garden fence.

On our row of five terraced houses, the Goulds lived next door to us. They were an elderly brother and sister—both unmarried and childless—a sweet and gentle pair, pillars of wisdom and grace. The sight of the siblings, with their silver hair and kind eyes, evoked a feeling of reverence. Mr Gould was always called "Mr Gould" but his sister was always known by her first name, Lois.

My mother told me that Lois was a spinster, using the word as a mark of respect and admiration for the choice Lois had made to remain single and childless. I was once told off for using this word by an editor, not realising that today it is considered a derogatory term. Yet in the 1960s, it had no such negative connotations, and my mother used the word to mean what the Cambridge Dictionary currently describes it as: "a woman who is not married, especially a woman who is no longer young and seems unlikely ever to marry." Simples. And I am described as a "spinster" on my marriage certificate - and that was in 1994. Maybe they use a different word on marriage certificates these days?

Mr Gould often smoked a pipe, its sweet aroma lingering in the air like a warm hug on a lazy summer afternoon. The fragrance of the tobacco carried on the gentle summer breezes would wrap around me as I played in the garden, creating an unforgettable sensory experience.

My mother enjoyed a natter with the Goulds over the garden gate, their voices carrying a soothing melody. The laughter that resonated into the garden was like a gentle lullaby, bringing a sense of joy to all who heard it. The touch of the weathered wooden gate, as they leaned against it, spoke of years of shared stories and connections.

Mr Gould and his sister Lois Gould, 1977, in our back garden in front of my beloved swing

The Goulds were the only ones we knew of in our street that had a piano. I only ever went into their home once as a child—a rare invitation—to play the piano. I could only play "Chopsticks". I don't think they were impressed.

Next to the Goulds dwelt Mr and Mrs Mac, a gracefully ageing couple whose children had long since flown the nest. Being more wealthy than the rest of us, their pristine home and garden exuded an air of prosperity, adorned with the latest mod-cons that whispered luxury. Mrs Mac was always telling us about their latest purchase - one such item was a teasmade which was quite a novel appliance to have in the 60s. They may have been elderly, but they were keen to embrace modern homeware.

Mrs Mac disclosed to my mother on several occasions that as the night settled in, Mr Mac would lovingly recite a customary bedtime phrase to her, "Good night, sleep tight, see you in the morning." It was a sweet refrain that never failed to bring her comfort as the sound of his gentle voice lingered in the air, weaving a sense of tranquillity amidst the night's embrace. Such were the simple things that brought ordinary people comfort.

Mrs Mac was skilled at crocheting, and she once made me a beautiful pale lemon bed jacket in an intricate lacy pattern. I loved it and wore it for many years; its comforting warmth was not only physical but also spoke of the love and care Mrs Mac had woven into every stitch.

Next door to the Macs were Mr & Mrs Lolley and their daughter Norma. Norma was four years older than me and always brought a smile to my face. We spent many happy hours in each other's company, our laughter filling the air. But more about her later.

The Lolleys' garden was a vibrant spectacle, showcasing an abundance of dahlias in every imaginable colour. However, the blooms were often covered for weeks to protect them, resulting in their back garden resembling a sea of paper bags.

Mr Lolley, a knowledgeable gardening enthusiast, also grew different types of vegetables. An enormous greenhouse stood proudly at the bottom of the garden, emitting a pleasant earthy smell that mingled with the scent of tomatoes. His marvellous shed was home to all kinds of amazing tools and gardening requisites. A lasting memory is being invited to tea and of the wonderful salads Mrs Lolley prepared with homegrown produce. And I well remember observing on Saturday mornings Mr Lolley enjoying his elevenses: a bacon and beetroot butty. I have yet to try this quirky combination; I'm sure it is quite delicious, with the pickled beetroot adding sharpness and sweetness to the bacon .

Mr Lolley—a motor car pioneer—owned a magnificent Rover; its sleek design and powerful engine were a testament to his passion. He was one of the first in the neighbourhood to transform his small front garden into a drive, allowing him to park his beloved vehicle off-road. The feeling of pride and innovation filled the atmosphere whenever Mr Lolley's Rover graced the driveway.

The Lolleys were also the first to have a telephone. They were very go-ahead in embracing such new technologies, and it was with great excitement that during the 70s, they also bought a tape recorder and cine camera. My father was not interested in such things, so it was with much fascination that I followed their pursuit of progress.

The last neighbours at the end of the terrace were the elderly Mr and Mrs White, a quiet, sweet-natured couple who kept themselves to themselves.

On the other side of our house, the elderly Mr and Mrs Smith neighboured us, and he had one of the allotments at the bottom of our gardens.

My mother, with a disapproving tone, labelled him a "dirty old man", and she warned me not to do cartwheels in a dress (thus revealing my knickers) when he was around. It remained a mystery as to how he acquired such a reputation, and in the event, he turned out to be quite harmless.

My little sis once daringly reached over the fence and snatched an enormous marrow which she chopped up for her mud pie, unaware that it was Mr Smith's prize vegetable. He was not well pleased. Such an event summed up the extent of drama in our street where nothing much happened.

Next to the Smiths lived old Edie. She was mentally unstable, often wandering the street in her dishevelled nightgown fluttering in the breeze, a cigarette perpetually dangling from her mouth. She would cry out using many expletives, her shouts piercing the quiet street. We accepted that she was angry - angry at someone or something, though the source of her anger remained a mystery, but the tension in her voice was palpable. She was harmless however and as children, we accepted her as she was including her effing and blinding.

Then there were the Lees: a mother and her son, Robert (or "Lyobert," as his mother called him), who couldn't "get a job anywhere" (or rather "lyob," as Mrs Lee called it, since she was unable to pronounce "job").

It might seem on the surface I am making fun of Mrs Lee with this disclosure, but I'm simply recording a fact that she —along with her speech impediment—was accepted without question as part of our neighbourhood community, and she was never judged, humiliated or treated unkindly because of it. My father loved her mispronunciations, and they only served to make us love her all the more.

My parents often used to stop and chat with Mrs Lee for a while if she was in her front garden doing some weeding. Her conversation always turned to her son. 'Our Lyobert can't get a lyob anywhere, he can't,' she lamented.

And so it was that Robert (Lyobert) was permanently unemployed—perhaps due to lack of education or because his background was originally from a traveller community, for, in the 1960s, the education of travellers was not on the government's radar at all, and they were a neglected community of people. We never found out, and it would have been rude to have asked, but my parents always enjoyed a natter with Mrs Lee, and had a strong sense of belonging with all our neighbours.

Directly opposite our house were Mr and Mrs Wells and their two daughters, Pamela and Lynda. They were the most well-off family in the street, and their home seemed like a palace with plush furnishings. They even paid to have all their ceilings artificially lowered, giving their rooms a more cosy atmosphere. My mother envied this alteration to their home after she was invited into the Wells' house to see the transformation.

When I was six years old, their eldest daughter, Pamela, came to play with me one day and tried to make me drink some Domestos bleach. But I blew the whistle to my mother—little snitch that I was—after Pamela went home. She was horrified and forbade me to ever play with her again, commending me for refusing to drink the bleach and for knowing that it was a dangerous substance.

Next to the Wells were Mr and Mrs Hamilton, two amiable pensioners, along with their adorable Yorkshire Terrier named Peppy (which my father insisted on calling Peppy-Poo-Pah).

Peppy—adorned with a little red bow on his head—seemed to be glued to Mrs. Hamilton, as she was rarely seen without him being carried under her right arm. As for Mr. Hamilton, he suffered greatly from heartburn. Neighbours just knew those sorts of things back then, you see.

Then there was Mr and Mrs Satchwell, who had several children and were a much poorer family.

Of Mr Satchwell, my father—who loved to mess around with songs and words—would sing around the house now and again, "Say! Mr Satchwell we're so proud of you for the way you're helping us to carry on…" to the chorus of the old George Formby song "Thanks Mr Roosevelt".

The reason as to why my father took to singing this praise of Mr Satchwell to George Formby's tune remains a mystery. Maybe Mr Satchwell had done some noble thing once for the street, but if so, I never found out what it was. More likely, it was my father just having a bit of fun in his comical manner - he loved daft songs.

Mrs Satchwell didn't escape my father's keen observation of grammatical errors in her speech. She spoke with a particularly enchanting brand of Birmingham accent, and one morning, as we were waiting at the top of Lockwood Road to get the bus to Digbeth coach station to go on one of our rare holidays, she spotted us on her way home from shopping.

'Where yow off to then?' she enquired jauntily, spying our suitcases around our legs.

'We're going on holiday to Tenby for a couple of weeks,' announced my father, 'we're getting the coach from Digbeth station.'

'Am ya?' she declared with surprise by way of question, 'enjoy yerselves then. Tara-a-bit.' ("Am ya" being interpreted as "are you?").

'Am ya?' repeated my father, laughing, as Mrs Satchwell waltzed off home. 'Am ya? What kind of British is that? Am ya sounds more like a vegetable than a question.' (His use of the word 'British' rather than 'English' was deliberate).

But "Am ya" had made his day. Another quirky grammatical curiosity for him to ponder.

This playfulness of my father manifested itself from time to time, and he loved to mimic some of the other neighbours, but it was all harmless fun and formed part of our community bonding. There was no malice in it, and we cherished the individuality of each and every neighbour.

My father's love of strange words, mispronunciations and wrong grammar is probably where I learnt my intrigue with them too. He often used spoonerisms and created his own words, phrases and nicknames. A favourite spoonerism of his was "ket the puttle on," (for "put the kettle on"), and he also enjoyed the juxtaposition of opposing and incongruous ideas.

My mother told me that I was once a target of his playfulness with words when I was a toddler. To my mother's annoyance, his nickname for me was Little Nellie Keltenbrunner. This was his play on the title of a 1940s film called "Little Nellie Kelly".

My father got untold pleasure from changing the word "Kelly" to "Keltenbrunner", for Keltenbrunner was a cruel, murderous Nazi and his brutality was in blatant contrast with me being an innocent and harmless two-year-old.

I was the polar opposite of the evil Keltenbrunner.

'Don't call her that, Les!' my mother would retort. 'Oh Les, stop calling her that name!'

But my mother's pleas just fell on deaf ears as the misnomer highly amused him.

And as for my father's impression of a camel chewing the cud, well, I'll leave the imagination of the reader to think on that, suffice it to say it never failed to make children and adults alike laugh out loud.

But I digress—so, back to our neighbourhood.

Diagonally opposite the Satchwells at the foot of Westcliff Place was Mr and Mrs Dodwell, an elderly couple who were just like all the other pensioners in our street - gracious, kind and gentle.

Mrs Dodwell had a walking disability, perhaps because of a

vitamin D deficiency in her childhood, for she was badly bow-legged. She was short and rotund, contrasting markedly against her tall, skinny husband. She was a helpful neighbour and very caring—almost like the matriarch of the whole street, taking us under her wing, like a grandmother, not only to me but to everyone.

Very early one winter morning, snow was falling thick and fast. Still, despite her difficulty in walking, she made the short journey through several inches of snow to every house in the street that had school-age children to inform the parents not to send their children to school. Snow was falling with flakes "as big as half-crowns," she said, and getting thicker. It had been announced on the radio that it would be getting worse, and it wasn't safe to venture out. These small gestures by Mrs Dodwell were always remembered by our family.

Wasdale Road was not just a street, but a tapestry woven with the threads of human connection. The sights, sounds, and feelings that filled our lives created a sense of belonging and community, making it a place we were proud to call home.

And so it was that the neighbourhood surrounding us sang with kindness, caring and acceptance in an understated manner, as did thousands of other working-class streets in Britain. The sense of community of our immediate neighbours was reassuring, where each member was valued and respected.

8. NAVY BLUE KNICKERS
AND LIBERTY BODICES

1963-64

My fingers and toes throbbed sore with pain from my chilblains as my mother and I waited at the bus stop. Our weekly visit to see my nan was over. Dusk was falling on the bitterly cold March afternoon as we made our way home.

'Let me rub your donnies to warm them up,' my mother cooed as she massaged my hands inside hers.

Every morning during winter, she bathed my chilblains in my urine to help make them better.

It didn't work.

I was blighted with chilblains throughout my childhood during the winter months. Exposure to the cold caused these itchy, red patches on fingers and toes to swell and cause pain. A traditional remedy for easing the discomfort of chilblains was to soak them in tepid urine. But I digress...

My maternal grandmother, Doris, lived in a small house on Birdbrook Road, Great Barr, and it was a long walk up Goodway Road to the number 33 bus, but I was never bored because I practised walking with my feet pointing straight out in front of me. I was prone to walking pigeon-toed.

'Walk with your feet pointing straight ahead, darling,' my mother gently advised, 'then you'll walk properly.'

After enduring an endless wait in the bone-chilling cold, we boarded the blue and yellow Birmingham Corporation open-ended bus. The icy wind swept through the vehicle, enveloping us in a draughty embrace. We had no choice but to settle at the back, as the front of the bus was already packed with passengers attempting to escape the chilly rear seats, and my mother would never sit upstairs - it wasn't easy navigating the winding stairs up to the top deck while the bus was moving, quite apart from the fact that the air up there would be thick with tobacco smoke.

Despite the frigid temperatures, I found solace in the bus rides. The sight of the ticket machine dangling from the bus conductor's neck fascinated me. With a simple turn of a handle, a tiny ticket materialised like magic. The conductor's uniform emitted a distinct, leathery oily odour. It was one of those whiffs from childhood that etch themselves into one's memory, even though it can never be physically relived again.

When we got off the bus in the city centre, we'd stop near New Street Station where the "baked potato man" sold his baked spuds and chestnuts from a cart.

The potatoes were black and charred with crispy skins served in a triangle paper bag with a twist of salt. But inside the hard skin was beautifully soft fluffy potato. There was never a more appetising aroma or a more delicious snack on cold days, warming mittened hands and the innards.

We then had another bus journey from the city centre to take us to the top of Lockwood Road in Northfield, gifting us another long walk down to Wasdale Road. I'd practice my walking technique or—when I was a little older—we would sing the pop song "Down Town". We loved the glamorous Petula Clark along with the picture she painted with the lyrics where the bright lights of the town invite you to forget all your troubles, forget all your cares "when you're DOWN TOWN!" we would chorus.

The song cheered my mother. It had been a difficult few years for her. She'd suffered a stillbirth in 1962 due to pre-eclampsia and also the loss of her father, Tom, a year later. During those dark days, she'd had me to look after, and this had given her the will to live. A social worker had visited after the baby loss and—finding my mother still in bed mid-afternoon with me happily playing by her side—had told her
that I should be taken into care.

My mother was horrified.

'Don't you DARE take her away from me!' my mother had

retorted. 'She's my only reason for living.'

She told me this many years later when I was an adult. I so wish I had put my arms around her and hugged her when she disclosed her baby loss experience, but I just sat and listened.

The baby, Diane, was full-term; my mother had carried her for almost nine months. She told me how she'd had pain and had to bang the bathroom wall with an iron to alert her neighbour to the need for help.

At the hospital, Diane was stillborn. And then she was gone. My mother must have wondered what they did with her baby after she was taken away.

Anyone who has known the pain of baby loss will understand the trauma that surrounds the experience.

She told me that after the birth in the recovery room, she'd had an overwhelming desire to hold a baby. Any baby.

'I'd like to hold a baby,' my mother asked one of the midwives.

This presented the midwife with a bit of a dilemma - would my mother abscond with a baby that wasn't her own?

However, a few moments later, my mother was holding a newborn baby boy—a black baby, and his mother had consented to the midwife's request.

'He was beautiful, Dawn,' my mother reminisced. 'He had big, round eyes that looked up at me as I fed him his bottle,' she recalled.

This may seem a politically incorrect thing to do these days - but what was the midwife to do? Ignore my mother's pain? Back then, stillborn and miscarried babies were whisked away from the mother. Thankfully, today, parents who suffer a baby loss are treated with more compassion and respect; they are given the choice to hold their baby and have a funeral if they wish, and even for babies lost before 24 weeks of pregnancy, parents can request a baby loss certificate .

But in 1962, there was nothing.

So it was a beautiful thing that the midwife (and the mother of the baby) did for my mother.

'I felt so much better after I'd held him,' she said.

This act of kindness was performed out of compassion for my grieving mother, and the midwife showed both compassion and wisdom within the limitations she faced.

I never learnt how my father felt about this loss; it was something he never discussed.

The weekly visits to my nan were always a highlight of my week for several reasons, but not least because there was an old upright piano in her front room. Like the rest of the furniture and the wooden doors in my nan's house, it was riddled with woodworm, but the piano's keys still produced clear notes, if a little twangy.

As I grew older, I sat down at the piano and taught myself to play the tune "Greensleeves". The sound of each note resonated through the room, filling the air with melodic beauty. I even experimented by adding a few matching notes with my left hand, creating a harmonious blend of sounds. "Chopsticks" was still a favourite ditty to play, but I found it somewhat crude; I felt "Greensleeves" was a little more classy.

In winter, the front room was as chilly as a refrigerator, for it was never lived in or heated. The cold seeped into my bones, but I hardly noticed it as my focus remained unwavering, and I poured all my concentration into the music. The room's crisp air mingled with the notes, creating an ethereal atmosphere.

Playing my nan's piano became a musical seed planted early in my life, a passion that blossomed late. I cherished the ability to play a simple tune and transform it into something pretty by picking out a few harmonious notes with my left hand.

On arriving home after our weekly visit, my mother would put on her "pinny" and cook what we called "tea", though, in fact it was dinner, the main hot meal of the day—meat and two or three veg—ready for my father's return from work.

The next morning, my chilblains were no better, and the Birmingham frost had drawn spiky patterns on our windows. The steam rose from my liberty bodice as my mother aired it in front of the coal fire.

The liberty bodice was an extra layer of warmth to be worn over my vest. It was a sleeveless fleecy cotton undergarment with rubber buttons down the front.

My mother had concerns about my health and was convinced that the liberty bodice reduced any chest infections. Like most mothers, she had health anxieties over her child. I was succumbing to frequent minor ailments and I can only think that the doctor got fed up with our many visits to the surgery.

'Well, she's not a gutter child,' was his verdict about my supposedly poor immunity and frequent colds, 'I'll prescribe a course of heat treatment.'

Unbeknown to my mother, this heat treatment (or "sunray therapy" as it was also called) was highly controversial at the time because it involved exposing children to ultraviolet light (the equivalent of putting them on a sunbed!), and some doctors questioned the procedure. I have wondered if it was the root cause of the three "in situ" melanomas I developed in my late 50s.

The heat treatment involved a course of weekly visits to the clinic for a group of (supposedly sickly) boys and girls stripping down to their pants, putting on grotesque goggles and sitting on hard benches in a darkened room which had a distinctive smell, while the UV lamps did their magic. We did look a sight.

On the subject of health, working-class children in 1960s Britain were more privileged than their counterparts in poorer countries, but the measles and mumps vaccines were still not available, and I contracted both diseases.

My mother told me that I nearly died from measles as an infant and I had to be kept in a darkened room to prevent me from going blind. Maybe my mother's health anxieties weren't unfounded.

Keeping warm during the winter months was a constant battle as there was no central heating, and only the living room was heated. To take the chill off our beds, my mother used a Glow Baby bed warmer, which was a light bulb inside a metal frame. It gave out a feeble amount of warmth, but we would snuggle under a thick feathered Eiderdown on top of our sheets and blankets, and we wore warm, fleecy nightwear with a woolly bed jacket to help ward off bedtime chills. Being cocooned under the weight of the blankets and thick Eiderdown was comforting, and sleep soon came, despite the cold.

'Now, you little bastards.'

I was playing my favourite morning game with my dolls. I'd lined them all up and was teaching them how to put their shoes on.

'Oh darling, you mustn't call them that, it's a bad word,' my mother gently corrected me, in her posh voice that she often adopted.

I actually don't remember this event, but my mother did and told me many years later how she'd heard me call my dolls "bastards" (in quite a plummy accent apparently), though she had no idea where I'd picked up the word, let alone speak it in Oxford English. She could only think that I'd heard my father use it once or twice (he could sometimes put on a posh accent now and again if the fancy took him), though he never swore or used any bad language when I was a child. Or maybe I'd heard old Edie use the word as she roamed our street in her nightie, with her fag hanging out of her mouth as she shouted expletives in her anger and sadness.

Swearing in public was not practised in our neighbourhood community at all, though we made an exception for Edie because of her illness. But generally, mild swearing was confined to the weekly edition of *Till Death Do Us Part*.

When I came home from school one day and used the word "shit", my mother was shocked and asked me where I'd learnt it.

'My new friend at school uses it,' I confessed.

'Well, it's a very naughty word, darling, and you mustn't say it. Don't play with her again,' I was told.

During weekday afternoons I'd enjoy *Watch With Mother*

programmes on our black and white television. My first love was Bill and Ben the Flowerpot Men because they had their own special language, using interesting words like "flobadop" and "bobop ickle weeeeed" (later condemned by educators for apparently preventing children from learning good English).

The late afternoon would drift into early evening when I'd anticipate my father coming home from work - might he bring me some sweets?

Then, lying on the settee, as the evening meal was being cooked, I would enjoy my soothers - not just one, but two. I'd suck one dummy, and stroke my eyebrows with the other. What a strange child I was.

'Woof woof!' barked my father. 'Woof woof!' echoed my mother. This was a favourite game to get me to eat my tea. We pretended to be dogs, and all three of us would be on all fours quadrupeding around the settee while they shovelled my food into my mouth. For some reason, I'd eat it if I imagined I was a hungry pooch. I most definitely was a strange child.

My preschool days eventually came to an end when I reached the grand age of five. My mother was adamant that I would be attending the Church of England School—St Laurence —rather than the infant school in Bellfield Lane just up the road.

I was equipped with a brown satchel, along with an exceptionally smart school uniform including a delightful beret, and three pairs of navy blue knickers (one to wash, one to wear and one to keep).

A special treat during my school years was a visit to Hughes shoe shop in Northfield. My mother insisted on buying Clarks shoes—it was a brand she trusted to ensure top quality, a good fit and to keep growing feet healthy. As we stepped into the shop, the scent of new leather filled the air, mingling with the subtle aroma of polished wood. The shop was filled with rows upon rows of shoe boxes and neatly arranged shoes on display, their shiny surfaces reflecting the soft glow of the overhead lights.

I was led to a plush chair, its velvety fabric inviting me to sink into its comforting embrace. As I sat on the chair, the shop assistant gently took each foot and placed it in a special contraption that measured the length and width. She did it with such care and tenderness that it gave me a warm glow inside. By allowing an extra half-size for growth, a pair usually lasted me several months.

The trek from Wasdale Road to St Laurence Infant School involved the long walk up Lockwood Road (more practice for keeping my feet pointing straight in my new shoes) followed by a short bus ride to the infant school in Great Stone Road. And yes, there really is a 'great stone' there (an ancient glacial boulder), and I'd meet my mother in front of it after school.

I was very fond of my brown satchel and the smart St Laurence school uniform in royal blue - but especially the stylish beret which I sensed was an elegant accessory. The boys wore caps.

However, I wasn't so keen on the St Laurence school logo: it was a griddle (or gridiron) symbolising the saint's painful and grisly martyrdom. We were all made aware of the meaning of the grid and that he was roasted to death on it.

The St Laurence School Logo.
The school still has the gridiron as the logo to this day

So, having started school, it was not only liberty bodices that were being aired in front of the fire, but now the thick pairs of navy blue knickers (required for PE lessons) and this undergarment also became a staple item as a stocking filler at

Christmas.

"Away in a manger, no crib for a bed..."

It was the middle of July and my mother was singing her favourite carol as I dozed off to sleep.

"Be near me, Lord Jesus, I ask Thee to stay close by me forever and love me I pray..."

Drifting off to sleep to her loving, dulcet tones was a comforting nightly ritual. She would sing this carol all year round.

"Bless all the dear children in Thy tender care..."

Despite my father being a Catholic, and my mother "Church of England" as she called it, neither of them attended church at all. My father often boasted throughout his life, "I'm a Catholic, I am," yet he never attended Mass once he'd left the Royal Navy. He did, however, have his own Requiem Mass at his funeral. Thankfully, the extreme polarity between Protestantism and Catholicism was lost on them and, therefore, a non-issue. Our family life never suffered one jot from my parents' religious labels—as that is all they were, just labels—and it never went any deeper than that. So ambivalent about religion were my parents that they never even had me or my sister "Christened".

The soothing tones of my mother's voice singing "Away in a Manger" was perfect lullaby music for a young child, and to this day, the carol brings a lump to my throat as I recall my mother's love and care as she sang me to sleep.

These things form my earliest memories.

I don't have much recollection of anything before that time, apart from a fuzzy vague memory of meeting many aunts and uncles on my father's side at my paternal grandmother's house in Bordesley Green. This came to a swift close on her death in 1963, when contact with some of my father's older siblings fizzled out.

My paternal grandmother, Rosina, was like the matriarch of

the family. Even from beyond the grave, she is like a magnetic force: the hub around which my paternal family revolves, linking her descendants many decades later, bringing 1st, 2nd and 3rd cousins into random contact on social media and in real life. We are all united in acknowledging her courage as she faced a hard life, raising a large family in such difficult circumstances.

"Pussy cat, pussy cat, where have you been?
I've been to London to visit the Queen.
Pussy cat, pussy cat, what did you do there?
I frightened a little mouse under her chair."

I was singing along to my Kidditunes 78 rpm record on my battery-operated toy gramophone I had seven of these records with all manner of popular children's songs and nursery rhymes, but I loved the green disc the best - simply because it was green, not black like all the rest.

It was playing these records that ignited a lifelong love of singing, and I spent hours playing, listening and singing along to them, learning the words by heart. Such an item was a sign of affluence for my parents, though many working-class children still did not enjoy such sophisticated toys. My parents were fortunate to have enough disposable income at Christmas and birthdays to lavish such gifts on me, their only child at that time, and I was blessed to benefit from their joy in giving.

9. SCHOOL

Clank clank clank clank clank…I ran the stick I'd found in the playground along the school railings during playtime, back and forth, back and forth. I liked the rhythmical sounds it made.

I wasn't making friends at St Laurence infant school—being shy—so finding a stick and running it up and down the railings seemed like a good idea to pass the time.

I didn't feel lonely, just solitary. But I was happy with that.

I was slow at learning and not the brightest child by any stretch, and I was too much of a dreamer.

First School Photo

St Laurence School in Northfield began in 1714 when the Rector of Northfield, Dr William Worth, ordered some books for his new charity school - a school for 20 boys.

In 1870, the State undertook responsibility for elementary education, and St Laurence came into the national system, with 114 children divided into two schools - Boys and Girls Juniors and Infants.

By the time I joined in 1964, there were 800 children divided between the two schools.

There are some interesting notes *From the Log Books* of St Laurence school:

Feb. 3rd, 1872
Deep snow, only 9 children present.

Nov. 10th, 1885
Had to send Harry F. home for School Pence which it now appears he has spent.

Feb. 2nd, 1886
John C. Very saucy to me this morning so punished him. It is very hurting to see children brought up to be impudent and stupid and it makes the teacher's task hard and thankless to have to strive at school to reform Character which are allowed to run to weeds at home and are actually encouraged in wrong-doing. There are very few parents of the Old English stamp left now.

Sept. 13th, 1886
Arthur H. Very lazy and as he had not done his lesson I kept him at school during dinner time. He, however, escaped through the window, and as he is a very wicked boy, and quite a character capable of ruining a class I sent word to his parents that I considered it best he should be placed under strict supervision.

...Thankfully, I was not aware of any such misdemeanours during my time at St Laurence in the 60s. We were a much more well-behaved lot.

Once I'd started school, I only visited my nan, Doris, during school holidays, but my mother continued her weekly visits during term time without me.

My nan had a darts board hanging on the back of the living room door, which got smattered with holes where the darts had missed the board, adding to the holes from the woodworm.

One afternoon, my mother was so engrossed in playing darts with her family that she forgot the time. She was supposed to be picking me up from school at 4 p.m. outside "the Stone" (aka, the glacial boulder).

I waited.

And waited.

All the other children and their parents drifted away.

I was the only one left.

Still, I waited, and waited.

I was calm and studied the stone.

I found a stick and ran it up and down the railings in front of the stone.

Clank clank clank clank clank it went.

I knew I must stay outside the stone and not go off with any "strangers". My mother had primed me many times to never, ever, under any circumstances, get into the car of a stranger, man or woman.

My mom would come eventually. I was convinced of that.

And she did.

I guess I had a lucky escape because it wouldn't have been difficult for a five-year-old girl to have been abducted by force from a quiet road. No one would have known.

I recall my mother almost running toward me and commending me for staying where I was. I can only imagine the anguish and sheer terror she must have felt on that bus journey to pick me up, wondering if I'd still be waiting for her.

It never happened again.

Despite my solitary time at infant school and not making any friends there, I was quite happy. I particularly enjoyed the daily drink of milk, which was given out in cute miniature milk bottles with a straw through the shiny silver top. This daily dose of full-fat milk—a source of calcium and vitamin D —was introduced into schools for all children in 1946, after an investigation in 1937 by top scientist and nutritionist John Boyd Orr revealed that there was a link between low income, malnutrition and underachievement in schools. Today, dairy milk has gone out of favour on several levels. How times change. I wonder what The Rt. Hon. The Lord Boyd-Orr would make of it?

Alongside enjoying a daily dose of full-fat milk, painting

colourful pictures on the large easels was my favourite activity, as well as taking part in the school plays:

All dressed up for our annual school play, circa 1966
(I am sitting cross-legged, bottom left)

However, it has to be said that, for me, the most cherished time at school was undoubtedly the afternoon nap - a blissful respite from the hustle and bustle. The cloakroom, filled with the pong of coats, PE kits and rubbery plimsolls, housed our small personal cushions, each delicately hanging on our designated pegs. With anticipation, we retrieved our cushions, feeling their softness between our fingertips, and carefully placed them on our desks. As the room grew quieter, the sound of rustling fabric filled the air, accompanied by the occasional yawn. Finally, we rested our weary heads on the cushions, surrendering to the drowsiness that enveloped us. This love for slumber has endured, as even today, the allure of the occasional afternoon nap beckons, embracing me with a sense of tranquillity.

"Jingle bells, jingle bells, jingle all the way, oh what fun it is to ride in a one old slopen sleigh, OH!" I sang the song with gusto, holding my mother's hand on the way home from school on the last day of term in December 1966, happily practising my walking technique, keeping my feet pointing straight out in front.

'Oh, darling, those aren't the right words. It's "in a one horse-**open** sleigh," sweetheart,' my mother informed me.

I was crestfallen—not because of my mother's correction, but because the image I'd had of an old sleigh that was sloping dashing through the snow was now defunct.

Never mind.

I scrambled up on one of the many large mounds of snow which people had shovelled under the trees to clear the footpath on Lockwood Road and shouted at the top of my voice.

'I'm the king of the castle and you're the dirty rascal!' ...a favourite chant of 60s children from those snowy mounds.

My mother helped me down, anxious that I would fall and crack my head open on the pavement. She always had a heightened awareness of danger and was prone to catastrophising, but then again, maybe she was right to be cautious. She lifted me down, and I could smell the familiar scent of her Crème Simon face cream...another childhood aroma gone forever.

Just as I started infant school, my mother landed a job at the Royal Orthopaedic Hospital in Northfield as a domestic cleaner. It was part-time employment where she was required to work from 5 p.m. until 8 p.m. for four evenings each week: Friday, Saturday, Sunday and Monday.

But what to do with me on Monday and Friday evenings?

My father didn't get home until after 6 p.m.

It was Mrs Dodwell, our kindly matriarchal neighbour, who came to the rescue, offering to look after me until my father got home. I spent many happy and contented hours with the Dodwells, being shown kindness and love. When Mrs Dodwell wasn't helping me to learn my times tables, I would be watching

TV with them, enjoying homemade cake, or sometimes playing with Mrs Dodwell's grandson, Colin, who was the same age as me, if he was well enough.

Colin was a sweet and gentle boy, and of fragile health, who loved his grandma dearly, spending as much time with her as possible. We were all aware that his home life wasn't a happy one. We never found out the full story as to why he was so very miserable at home, but Mrs Dodwell loved, nurtured and nursed him during his frequent illnesses.

He later died in her arms when he was 11 years old.

Mrs Dodwell's curtains were drawn for weeks (a custom often practiced in the 60s after a death in the family).

After a while, I moved up to St Laurence Church of England Junior School. Back then, school hours were longer, and we didn't leave school until 4 p.m. Unthinkable these days when pupils leave school at 3 p.m.

School was where my love of singing was also nurtured. One of my earliest memories is sitting cross-legged in my first year in the junior school, singing the hymn "God is Love, His the Care". It was a brand new hymn back then, and the teacher taught us to sing it, line by line, as she accompanied us on the piano.

School assemblies, where the Lord's Prayer would be recited each morning, were also great sing-alongs to familiar Anglican hymns. "All Things Bright and Beautiful" was a popular all-year-round hymn, alongside seasonal hymns such as "We Plough the Fields and Scatter" in the autumn, or "There is a Green Hill Far Away" at Easter.

At Christmas, it would be carols, where the children sometimes changed the words, and we all sang with gusto. Shepherds washing their socks by night was a favourite, and my father was doubled-up when I sang to him the school version of "We Three Kings of Orient Are" where there was "one on a scooter beeping his hooter following yonder star." He thought it was ace. The teachers turned a deaf ear to these childish whims, and none of us were reprimanded.

I also excelled at Country Dancing, where girls and boys danced together as couples. We danced and pranced to traditional country dance music, performed in sets, where the dance sequences ensured everyone danced with everyone else. We all had to do it, whether we liked it or not. But I did like it.

I became more sociable and made a few friends, but was still fairly dim academically, and I was placed in the lowest stream during my final year.

The school provided a good standard of education that had a warm and happy atmosphere, and I am grateful for it, but it was a school where the children of working-class parents could sometimes be discriminated against, and they were also assumed to be of lower intelligence or ability.

A vivid memory I have as an eight-year-old is when two boys in my class were emigrating to Australia. One boy was from a middle-class family, and our teacher—a Miss Turner—bought him a camera as a leaving gift.

The other boy, Malcolm, was working-class, and Miss Turner let him give out the milk bottles as a special leaving gift.

We all noticed it.

That difference.

It was almost subconscious, but we knew whose families were better off and whose families were poor.

It was in Miss Turner's class that she pounced on me during one lesson, pulling me up roughly by the arm from my chair and smacking the backs of my legs for something I was not guilty of (talking loudly). Another child had been talking loudly, but she didn't believe me. This injustice greatly affected me emotionally. My parents were quite concerned as I became very withdrawn afterwards.

'What's wrong, darling?' My mother persisted in getting to the bottom of my low mood, and I eventually told her what had happened. Even to this day, I feel I have to justify myself over things with long explanations, and I often think the root cause stems from this event.

Occasionally, the pupils would attend St Laurence Church for a service situated on the other side of the Bunbury Road. We had to form a line—boys on the outside, girls on the inside— as we walked side by side the short distance from the school to the church. It was considered proper etiquette for the boys to walk on the outside nearest the traffic, protecting us girls as we walked on the inside.

During our final year at primary school, we were taught how to write italic lettering with genuine italic pens and ink. I greatly enjoyed forming the elegant, sloping letters. It was therapeutic and absorbing.

I sat next to a sweet-natured boy called Daniel, who had a disability. His speech was badly impaired, and he wasn't easy to understand; plus, his walking was lopsided, and he often dribbled. The school assumed he was thick, hence putting him in the lowest stream with the rest of us dim wits.

He was a quiet boy, and I enjoyed sitting next to him, especially as we were both introverts, so it suited us both just fine. Due to his coordination difficulties, he often got the ink everywhere when we were practising our italic handwriting, including over his clothes, all over his hands, and many smudges on the paper. Good job we didn't have ink in the inkwells which were cradled on our 1950s desks - by the 60s we were using italic pens which had ink refills inside the pen itself, but they could be very temperamental and leak.

Our class also learnt some French.

The school employed a mature French lady to visit us once a week to teach us the language. She was an exceedingly elegant woman who wore stylish clothes and had blond coiffed hair formed into an impeccable beehive bun.

Teaching 11-year-olds French was perhaps rather visionary of Birmingham Education Authority in 1970. Maybe they'd foreseen closer ties with Europe, especially with decimalisation looming.

The first thing she taught us was our own name in French.

It got us all hooked.

It was personal now.

My name, Dawn, is *Aurore* in French.

I loved it.

Aurore. It sounded so…French.

'*Je m'appelle Aurore*', I would mutter, '*Je m'appelle Aurore*'.

It was otherworldly. Like having a new identity.

Glamorous and different.

I was no longer a working-class kid from a council estate in Birmingham called Dawn Smith. I was *Aurore.*

But that simple thing that sparked my love of the French language. I found it a very musical language, and it sang to my heart.

I do not doubt that our teacher, Mr Parry, did his level best to prepare us for our Eleven Plus examination, which all children in their final year of primary school had to take. This standardised test was used to assess verbal and non-verbal reasoning, mathematics, English components, cognitive ability and academic achievement. Introduced in 1944, it was designed to determine the type of school a student should attend after primary education: a grammar school, a technical school or a secondary modern school.

It was an alien concept for parents to pay for private lessons to get their children through this challenging exam in the 70s, and as we were in the lowest stream, it was assumed that we would all fail.

And we did.

Except for Daniel.

Despite his physical disability, his mental capacities were bang on cue, and he outshone us all.

The school got that one wrong.

Well done, Daniel.

A school leaving trip to the capital city was believed to be in order by the school governors as part of our all-round education. My parents were happy to pay the £11 fee for me to go to London, so off I went.

We stayed four nights at a hostel in Clapham Common and visited all the big sights, including Buckingham Palace, Madame Tussauds, London Zoo, 10 Downing Street, and London Bridge amongst other venues - it was a tight schedule.

My parents bought me a cheap camera for the trip, and I still have the blurry black and white photos illustrating a short diary I wrote. It was a good trip and a valuable experience to visit the landmark sites in the capital city, bringing the world-famous venues to life in our minds. We each had to write a short project about our visit.

My Visit to London

When I was 11, I went on a school leaving trip to London, for 4 days.

I had a good time visiting all the famous places.

Each day, we would have our breakfast, and then set out to tour London. We would have a packed lunch, containing sandwiches, apple or orange, chocolate, and a fruit pie, and a drink. We had a cooked meal out in different restaurants. The 'Golden Egg' was my favourite restaurant.

Then we would return to the hostel, watch T.V. then to bed. But we never got to sleep early because we had midnight feasts and played games in our rooms, which 6 to 8 shared.

There were about 38 of us altogether.

Three of my school friends on London Bridge
Taken with the cheap camera my parents bought me

I was disappointed that I failed my Eleven Plus because I'd had my heart set on attending Shenley Court Comprehensive School in Weoley Castle, but I had to settle for Colmers Farm Secondary School in Rubery instead.

As it turned out, Colmers Farm was the best school I could have attended, and I thrived there.

It was at Colmers that I learnt to read music, which enriched and changed my life.

10. NORMA

"It's on yer shoe!" we chanted in unison as we leaned on the front gate. The random passer-by glanced down at his shoes and carried on.

We sniggered.

It was an overcast summer's Saturday afternoon in 1968, and after eating a bag of sherbet pips, me and Norma were playing her favourite game (one which she'd made up) called "It's on yer shoe".

I wasn't so sure about this tomfoolery as to my mind, I thought it was fibbing to tell someone there was something on their shoe when there wasn't, but Norma enjoyed taunting them with this misinformation. She enjoyed a prank and a practical joke now and again, and I fell into line with the skylarking as I had to concede: it was rather fun watching the occasional passer-by look down at their footwear to see if something really was on their shoe.

They fell for it every time.

Norma was the daughter of Mr & Mrs Lolley, who lived three doors down, and she was four years older than me. Her sense of humour and fun was timeless. I was never aware of the age gap in our friendship, which lasted many years into adulthood.

We spent hours and hours in each other's company, usually playing Monopoly. Why we enjoyed playing that long, boring game, I have no idea, but we loved it. I think it was the little green and red plastic houses that did it - along with the mysteries of the Community Chest cards.

Norma and her parents, Olive and Norman, were physically voluptuous people and had voluptuous personalities to go with it. They were kind and generous, often inviting me to delicious teas (aka "dinner" - but in Birmingham, the main meal of the day was called "tea").

They were warm and welcoming, their benevolence overflowing as they showered our family with friendship. We were once all invited to Sunday lunch at the country home of their eldest daughter, Pat. We eagerly embarked on this adventure in Mr. Lolley's enormous Rover, our senses tingling with anticipation.

'Ooh goody goody gumdrops, we're going for a ride in a great big car!' I chanted, my voice filled with excitement, as we all piled in, squashed like sardines in the roomy back seat. No seatbelts were required, so we packed ourselves in.

The countryside awaited us, a rare treat for city dwellers. The scent of fresh air and cow dung filled our nostrils through the front vent windows of the Rover, and the vibrant colours of nature dazzled our eyes.

As soon as we arrived, Norma took the lead, showing me around the farm as we explored gates, yards, and fields.

And then we saw him in the distance, eyeing us up.

Our blissful day out was momentarily interrupted by the thunderous sound of a bull's hooves.Boy, did we run for our lives.

We only just made it.

As soon as Norma was 17, she learnt to drive and bought herself a bright yellow Ford with a black roof, complete with a nodding dog on the rear shelf. It was her pride and joy, and we often went for rides in it on Saturdays to local beauty spots such as Stratford.

We once embarked on a delightful adventure to Alton Towers, where we hired a rowing boat, the sun casting a golden glow on the sparkling river. Birds chirping and water gently lapping against the boat created a soothing melody as we glided downstream, surrounded by graceful weeping willows swaying in the breeze.

Lost in wonder and laughter, with Norma rowing me through the willow branches, time slipped away unnoticed until

Norma glanced at her watch. Panic washed over us as we realised we had exceeded our allotted half hour. We were horrified and, being short of money, couldn't face the prospect of rowing back to the quay to pay the extra bucks.

Oh no.

We couldn't do that.

So Norma decided she'd pull into the riverside bank and we'd get out and abscond.

I got out of the boat first, and Norma followed, abandoning the oars. With one leg on the bank and one leg in the boat, the boat decided it was going back into the river, with Norma doing the splits. She fell backwards into the bank, mud and all. After scrambling to her feet we scarpered before anyone could trace the empty boat now drifting aimlessly downstream with no one in it...

11. LITTLE SIS

My sister, Elizabeth, was born on the 30th August 1967.

My mother spent several days in hospital after the birth as women did in those days, enjoying a rest and being waited on - though she was most disappointed that she didn't get a bottle of stout each day as she had done when I was born eight years earlier. She'd been so looking forward to that special treat. It was thought that stout helped to replace iron in the blood, but maternity wards stopped issuing it during the 60s.

Early in the mornings before he left for work, my father took me around to our elderly neighbour, Mrs Mac, who was looking after me. I used to love my Ready Brek, but Mrs Mac was clueless about how to make it, and it was the consistency of thin soup. Nevertheless, her offer of help during my mother's confinement was an act of neighbourly kindness.

I was glad when my mother came back home with my little sister, though I was so put out by this interloper that my mother had to keep me off school for a week so that I could help to look after the newcomer, changing nappies, dressing her and bonding with my tiny sibling.

My mother had bought a new Silver Cross pram (she always had good taste in selecting the best brands), and pushing it up Lockwood Road in the late summer sun certainly encouraged me to enjoy the new baby. I suppose being the only child for eight years, it was a bit of a shock. My mother's plan worked, however, and I settled down.

When Elizabeth was a toddler, she caused us all a dreadful fright. An open pin went missing. My mother's vigilant observation of this fact caused her to take the drastic decision to take my sister to Selly Oak Hospital as she was convinced Elizabeth had swallowed it.

'It's impossible,' was my father's verdict on the idea that

a toddler could swallow a small open safety pin. 'She'd have choked trying to swallow that. You must be mistaken,' he said.

'I'm telling you, Les, the pin was on that table right there,' retorted my mother, pointing to the table to reinforce her knowledge. 'I turned my back for a few seconds, and now it's gone! I've looked everywhere for it. I'm taking her to Selly Oak Hospital right now,' she told him.

'You're wasting your time, there's no way she could physically swallow an open pin.'

But my mother was right.

The X-ray showed the open pin as clear as day in her stomach. We were all amazed that Elizabeth had survived swallowing an open pin, with no ill effects. She came home after an operation, the pin safely removed and presented to us as a keepsake by the hospital in a tiny glass jar which we kept for many years, with the pin rusting over time. Elizabeth still has the scar on her tummy.

On a different note, I learnt that sisters could be quite useful to cover up one's embarrassment, such as when I fell over one icy morning, and grabbed my sister's hand muff to pull her over with me so I wouldn't look such a fool. Now, that was not a nice thing to do, was it?

Little Sis
- on our back lawn with her Tiny Tears doll...and those
ugly garden palings behind her...
(Mr Lolley's wonderful enormous greenhouse and shed in the rear,
and the great oak tree in the playing field in the background)

'Things that go bump in the night, shouldn't really give one a fright; it's the hole in each ear, that lets in the fear. That, and the absence of light!'

Our dad was reciting one of his favourite Spike Milligan poems after he had finished telling us one of his made-up stories just before bedtime. Making up stories was an excuse for him to get creative with unusual names.

He captivated us with a vivid tale he spawned, weaving a tapestry of sights and sounds. Our eager ears absorbed the story of Mr Bigglesworth, a man whose greenhouse overflowed with the vibrant colours of tomato plants. Yet, within this horticultural haven lurked an unwanted visitor: Septimus Spider. The pungent scent of earth and plant life enveloped our senses as we imagined Mr Bigglesworth's futile attempts to rid his sanctuary of the unwanted arachnid. With each word, our eyes widened, eagerly embracing the allure of the quirky names "Bigglesworth" and "Septimus" as if they possessed a mystical power to draw us deeper into the enchanting world of the story.

And so it was, my little sister and I grew up together, each with our own childhood memories. She gained a reputation in our family for picking out winners at Grand Nationals—a feat she accomplished several times over the years.My father wasn't a betting man, but he did have a flutter once a year on the Grand National, allowing me and little sis to pick a horse each. At the grand age of seven, her little finger went down the list of horses and stopped at "Red Rum".

'That one,' said little sis as she showed my father which horse she'd chosen.

He couldn't believe it when it won.

'She's dead jammy,' my mother said after the race as she gave my sister her winnings, 'picked it out, just like that.'

12. PETS

In the 60s, nearly everyone's home had the obligatory "budgie", and the sound of chirruping budgerigars in people's living rooms was a familiar backdrop - and a rather irritating one at that.

We had a canary called Joey, who chirruped away all day. I gave Joey a little treat one sunny summer afternoon and took his cage outside and swung it around and around faster and faster. I was the hub of a fairground roundabout, and Joey was enjoying a lovely ride. The velocity of my spinning caused one of the glass slides at the side of the cage to fly out, then Joey flew out and flew away (we never found him, and he never came back), and my mother's asthma flew off with Joey. We realised then she had an allergy to birds' feathers.

When I was about five, my parents got a sweet black puppy, and we called him Rex. I do not recall what breed he was, if any, or where they got him from. In those days, you could buy animals from pet shops, and the popular novelty song "How Much is That Doggie in the Window" was a frequent ditty my mother would sing as she dusted the furniture or polished the brasses on the fire surround with Brasso. I'm glad those days are over for animals.

But poor Rex didn't stand a chance.

My father took Rex out for a walk before he'd had his distemper vaccine. Our sweet puppy contracted the disease, and his life was cut short. My mother was angry about it for many years after, blaming my father for taking our pup for a walk before it was safe. It seems my father hadn't believed the risk was real, thinking that a short walk wouldn't do any harm. I still feel sad about it to this day. Rex deserved better care.

Two other pets came into our lives. Tipsy was a tabby cat and brought us feline interest, intrigue and pleasure - apart from when she went missing in the middle of a snowy winter. We were all heartbroken at her disappearance.

But against all the odds, she returned to us—thin and bedraggled—and recovered, living to a good old age.

In the mid-70s, we acquired a gerbil—called Pip—from a pet

shop. He was a lively creature that we were fond of but unable to cuddle due to his boundless, wriggly energy. He disgraced himself by escaping from his cage one night, chewing through the radiogram wires, ruining it, and putting an end to our enjoyment of recorded music. The radiogram was one of our prized possessions, but alas, it was sadly relegated to being a neglected piece of furniture in the conservatory, where bits and bobs were kept. It never played another record or tuned into a radio station ever again after the onslaught of those sharp, rodent gnashers.

Pip was then condemned to live in his cage in the shed, and it was a sad day when we found him dead one snowy morning. Whether it was the cold or old age, we never found out, but I felt bad about abandoning the creature to such a fate in a cold shed.

However, it was an injured pigeon that my mother grew particularly fond of. She named him Brownie—due to his distinctive brown and white colouring—and Brownie would come into our kitchen every day for a short while, for some food and to sit on a perch over a bucket for his droppings to go into.

My mother became greatly attached to Brownie, looking for him every morning, and I sensed that she somehow viewed this visitation of the bird as some kind of sign that her deceased father was watching over her. Brownie eventually made a recovery and disappeared from our lives.

Generally, owning pets was not something that many people did in our street. The Lolleys had two tabby cats, which they kept safely attached to long leads when outdoors. They never let them roam freely for fear of them getting run over. But despite their restrictions, they were contented kitties enjoying much pampering.

The Hamiltons and their Yorkshire Terrier, Peppy (aka "Peppy-Poo-Pah" as my father called him), were the only other couple who had a pet.

13. GAMES AND THINGS

Do you want a cigarette Sir?
  No Sir
  Why Sir?
Because I don't smoke Sir,
Why Sir?
Well Sir,
  Because I've got a cold Sir.
  Where do colds come from?
  From the North Pole Sir.
  Whatcha doing there Sir?
  To catch a Polar Bear Sir,
  O. U. T. spells out Sir out Sir out Sir OUT!

This strange, mildly poetic chant was a great favourite game of mine.

It was chanted while standing with one's back to a wall, swinging a tennis ball in an old stocking from left to right against the wall in time to the rhythm of the poem.

On the word "Sir", the ball had to go under the left leg lifted. My father banned the game because the thud thud thud of the ball hitting the wall drove him nuts (though eventually it was banned in schools as being politically incorrect for some reason - though I'm not sure on what grounds, which only reinforces my era).

One of the sweetest things about growing up in the 60s was a childhood free from electronic games and devices. We used our imaginations and played with anything and everything we might find lying around. Despite having a nice collection of decent toys such as Barbie dolls, I much preferred more natural and earthier odds and ends to play with, which I found in the yard, shed or rubbish dump, requiring some inventiveness and creativity.

One of my favourite games involved playing houses in the backyard, where the mop was my best friend, and I would tie its stringy "hair" in a ponytail. I'd "cook" a dinner: bits of wood were meat, stones were potatoes, grass and weeds were the veg - all with a good helping of muddy "gravy".

The vibrant game of hopscotch was a beloved pastime for young girls in the neighbourhood. The pavement outside our front gate and beyond was a kaleidoscope of colourful squares made by thick strokes of chalk. The air carried the faint scent of dust and imagination as we giggled and skipped our way through the game. The sound of our laughter and the soft tapping of our shoes against the pavement filled the air, creating a symphony of joy and innocence.

Another favourite outdoor toy was my beloved space hopper. I was like a bouncing bunny as I sprang my way up and down our long back lawn, sometimes missing the mark and ending up rebounding backwards onto my butt.

From a young age, making daisy chains in the summer months would occupy us for half an hour or so as our nimble thumb nails made a cut into the daisy stems to thread them through each other. The dexterity required for this task must match any texting on a modern device perhaps.

A favourite game in the playground at school was British Bulldog. This is another 60s game which is now banned, but all I remember about it is that it involved a lot of running back and forwards from one side of the playground to the other, and it also involved both boys and girls. Usually, our games segregated us: skipping for girls, marbles for boys, but British Bulldogs was for everyone and brought us together.

A game called Stuck in the Mud was a popular playground pastime, and for girls, other activities involved jumping over elastic or a long piece of washing line swung back and forth as we chanted "Elec-tric wires! Elec-tric wires!" over and over again. We each took our turn to jump the wire and if it touched you, you were out.

These simple games kept us occupied throughout school playtimes and also served to keep us relatively fit, healthy and slim with lots of running and jumping.

Bonfire Night had a special aura each year. None of us children were educated as to who Guy Fawkes was or the history surrounding it. We were told he'd tried to blow up the Houses of Parliament, but as for the reasons behind it, they were never dissected or discussed. It was just a great family time which we looked forward to. The anticipation built weeks before, making and stuffing a Guy out of old clothes and building a big bonfire. Then on the big night itself, potatoes would be baked and chestnuts roasted in silver foil in the fire, while our dads let off cheap fireworks. The Catherine wheels were my favourite, although they often ended in a damp squib.

I was in my late 30s when I learnt the grim truth and reality of Guy Fawkes and Bonfire Night, but as children growing up, it was simply a tradition filled with fun, laughter and wonder.

"Run rabbit, run rabbit, run, run, run
Don't give the farmer his fun, fun, fun
He'll get by without his rabbit pie
So run rabbit, run rabbit, run, run, run."

My mother's melodic voice would often fill the air, carrying the sweet nostalgia of this 1930s song. Gathered together in the evenings, our voices intertwined in unison as the sound reverberated through the walls of our cosy home. These musical moments, led impromptu by our parents, created a symphony of togetherness.

On Saturday mornings, the sound of the radiogram would hum to life (before Pip the gerbil chewed the wires, that is), as the LP (Long Playing record) filled the room with the lively tunes of the band of the Royal Marines playing spirited marches. The vibrant melodies would dance through our ears, inspiring my father to take the lead, marching us around the settee.

'Qui——CK MARCH! Left, right, left, right…' he ordered as we followed him around the living room.

He had done some marching in the Royal Navy. The marches he played every Saturday stirred deep memories in him, and he enjoyed involving us, getting us "in on the act" (as he would have said). With each step, the creaking of the wooden floorboards beneath our feet echoed in rhythm with the music. My sister and I, giggling with delight, followed his lead, arms and legs in sync, feeling the energy pulsate in our veins.

Then, the familiar sound of the high-pitched whistle of the kettle boiling on the gas stove would pierce the air, followed by the aroma of Bird's Mellow Coffee enveloping the room as my mother prepared a milky beverage, mingling with the melodies and laughter. It's a brand of coffee I wouldn't touch with a barge pole these days, but it was considered a luxurious drink back then. Coffee was not widely consumed by working-class people - their preferred hot drink was tea. But a weak, mild and milky coffee at weekends was considered a luxury, and its warmth embraced us, enhancing the sense of comfort and love that filled our hearts.

As my sister and I grew older, the card game Solo was a firm favourite in our family. Solo is a relatively complex card game that our father taught us to play. He loved it. We played the game so often without shuffling the cards that they fell into a pattern, enabling several of us to achieve a "Grand Slam", including myself on more than one occasion, much to my delight. My father loved the intricacy of this card game and also the names of the different tricks such as *Misère* and *Abundance* - these words delighted his sense of language.

In these precious moments, our family bonded over such simple pleasures. The sights of smiles and laughter, the sounds of music and footsteps, the smell of powdered coffee - these small things that cost very little, gifted us the feeling of unity and created a tapestry of cherished memories that would forever remain etched in our minds.

14. CHITTERLINGS AND THINGS

"Ying tong, ying tong, ying tong, ying tong, ying tong diddle I po! Ying tong, ying tong, ying tong diddle I po! Diddle I po! Yeeeeee...," my father warbled in a silly nasal voice as he washed his pork chitterlings on a Saturday morning.

He loved the 'Ying Tong Song' by the Goons. It was one of his favourite bonkers songs, appealing to his love of nonsense words.

Chitterlings were a cheap and nutritious food, though my mother wouldn't eat them and neither would I, but my father loved them. He washed these pig intestines thoroughly under running cold tap water, and boiled them with onions in a mild vinegary brine; the acrid odour would linger in the air many hours after he'd finished eating them...yet another childhood odour now gone forever - but good riddance to it!

Often, the vinegary stink would mingle with the fresher smell of my father's snotty handkerchiefs boiling in Daz washing detergent in an old, giant saucepan, filling the kitchen with steam during winter months.

My father was somewhat old school when it came to food. He loved the cheap off-cuts, and often he would venture into the market at the Bull Ring in Birmingham city centre and buy jellied eels, chitterlings, pig trotters, tripe, or cooked meats such as brawn in jelly, or sliced tongue.

Another favourite food of his was mussels, which he would buy regularly from the market in the Bull Ring. Again, he would clean and prepare them while singing happy songs and boil them up, then eat them cold for supper with lashings of salt, pepper and vinegar, swilled down with draught beer from the local "outdoor". Occasionally, my father would bring home some periwinkles for me - which I picked out of their tiny shells using a cocktail stick.

Vinegar was a familiar smell in our home. My father would cook his pigs' trotters in water and vinegar, and these cheap, nutritious foods gave him immense joy to eat. They were succulent and savoury.

His other favourite food was jellied eels which he'd suck deliciously (he loved the jelly), swilled down yet again with a pint or two of bitter from the local "outdoor" just up the road.

A trip to the outdoor was a Friday evening ritual: my father would carefully rinse out a couple of empty lemonade bottles, and, holding my hand in his, we embarked on our journey up the road with the sound of our footsteps striking against the pavement.

At the shop—aka, the "outdoor" that sold draught beer— the air was heavy with the earthy aroma of beer, as the shopkeeper filled the bottles with the frothy liquid, the gentle hiss of carbonation tickling my ears. A bag of crisps and some dandelion and burdock for me completed the purchase, along with a packet of ten Gold Leaf cigarettes and a bag of pork scratchings for my father. These tough, greasy porcine treats, bristling with coarse pig hairs, demanded the strength of healthy teeth to conquer their crunchy texture. My father loved them.

As we walked hand in hand, my father would bounce his hand up and down, a playful cue for me to skip, and with each skip, my heart soared, my feet lightly tapping against the ground, creating a symphony of joyful pitter-patter.

Tinned foods were a staple part of a working-class diet in the 1960s. Tinned ham, tinned strawberries and tinned cream, tinned salmon for special occasions, tinned corned beef, and faggots or Fray Bentos tinned pies. These are foods which I never bought when I had my own home, apart from the odd tin of salmon. I think my generation began to associate these foods with a poorer standard of living - we wanted different eats. We craved more exotic delicacies like spinach and ricotta enchiladas, or lasagne.

Many other staple foods, however, were more nutritious. Eggs were a firm favourite for adults and children alike and were called "chooky eggs" when we were small - though we never knew why.

'Eat your chooky egg, and dip your bread and butter soldiers in the yolk,' would be spoken by way of a command to encourage us to eat.

I've only recently learnt that "chook" is an informal Australian word for hen, so how it made its way up to the northern hemisphere to working-class England to describe eggs I have no idea.

It was the humble "chooky egg" which was one of my father's chief pleasures, as he would occasionally have a "prairie oyster" where he would crack two raw egg yolks into a cup and shower them in Worcester sauce, salt and pepper. He'd down it in one go. Quite where he got this concoction from, I have no idea - it was possibly a throwback to his navy days where this egg combination was thought to cure a hangover if some brandy was added, though he rarely had too much drink unless he went boozing with his brothers. He just used to enjoy his eggy "oysters" as a treat - a somewhat dubious habit because of the risk of salmonella poisoning, but he was good on it.

My father loved making his home-cooked "spaghetti bolognese" - but it was nothing like the proper Italian version at all. It was simply minced beef with an Oxo cube thrown in, water, and a squirt of tomato puree, boiled up and served with long, plain spaghetti sprinkled with Parmesan cheese out of a plastic shaker. It was a cheap, easy meal, and he loved it, though we weren't so keen as it was bland, and the texture was most unappealing. On his spag bol days, my mother would prefer a nice piece of halibut from Flowerdews on the Bristol Road.

He was brought up on rabbit stew (bones and all), but I never knew him to cook a rabbit stew. Ever. It was not on his menu, perhaps because it was too much of a reminder of his poverty-stricken childhood. Meats such as beef, as well as lamb and even pork, represented more affluence.

It was while his mother (my grandmother - Rosina) was preparing a rabbit stew that my father earned his nickname *Parsley Darlin'*. While Rosina chopped parsley from the garden to add flavour to the stew, he had once asked, 'What's that, Mom?'

'It's parsley, darlin', she said. But my father thought that's what it was called—parsley darlin—and so one day when she was chopping it again, he'd asked, 'Is that parsley darlin what you're chopping up?'

And so it was from that time on, his nickname was *Parsley Darlin'*.

Pork belly and pork bangers (sausages) were another of my father's favourite foods. He'd often eat a few bangers for supper. One warm, balmy September evening as dusk fell, he was cooking some juicy sausages under the grill, and the back door was wide open, whereupon a daddy long legs flew in straight under the grill and was cremated on top of one of the sausages. Well, it would, wouldn't it? That vivid memory still lingers in my mind and surfaces every year when these critters inevitably find their way into our home, along with large velvety bobowlers, which my mother hated. Appearing suddenly at dusk, these large, ugly brown moths whirred around the lights and would make my mother furious. How dare they come into our home.

One dish my father particularly enjoyed was one he picked up from his navy days: stewed lamb's kidneys in a rich gravy on fried bread. Quick, easy and highly nutritious, even I enjoyed this filling, tasty breakfast. It is the one childhood meal that I often cook today for brunch (except I have the kidneys on toast and ditch the fried bread).

Breakfasts on school days were usually beans on toast, or Ready Brek with a banana or an apple sliced in. My mother was fastidious about sending us to school with a hot meal in our stomachs come rain or shine. "Three hot meals a day," was her mantra, as was her mother's before her, and no doubt going back generations. Food is fuel, and no matter how poor people were, a hot meal was known to be essential for good health.

Occasional rice puddings made with full-fat milk were a firm favourite, with the belief that they were nourishing. They were cooked in the oven for at least an hour, ensuring a lovely dark skin on top. The pudding—skin and all—was eaten with relish, whether hot or cold. Lactose-free diets were unheard of.

We usually only had puddings on a Sunday, and in summer it would be tinned strawberries and thick tinned cream sprinkled with sugar. I particularly enjoyed this pudding and after I'd eaten most of it, I would mix the syrup from the strawberries with the thick cream to form a pale pink sugary liquid, adding to the decay of my poor molars.

Sterilised milk was regularly used and we had one pint of "Sterra" a week—delivered by our milkman on his trusty milk float—as well as daily deliveries of pasteurised (or "pass" as we called it), in glass bottles.

'D'you want sterra or pass in your tea?' was a frequent question. If you were feeling hungry, it was always sterra. It somehow felt more filling and had a distinctive sickly sweet taste.

'Birds do it, bees do it, even educated fleas do it, let's do it...'

This time, my mother's voice warbled one of her favourite melodies as she sliced cucumber, tomatoes and a Spanish onion for a tantalising bowl of pickled summer salad to accompany cheese or ham.

The song always made her giggle. Even though it was about falling in love, I think she saw a saucier side to the song.

The method of preparing this simple savoury and vinegary treat seemed to go out of favour from the early 70s onwards, but it was popular with the older generation.

One summer afternoon, I was invited by Norma and her parents to visit her elderly grandmother on the other side of town. She was a gentle lady in her nineties who had long silver-white hair falling to her waist. Norma and I—nosy parkers that we were—found a large bowl of this mild, tasty pickle in her nan's pantry. Its savoury scent made our mouths water, and we helped ourselves to some of it. Well, quite a lot of it, in fact.

It was irresistible.

We kept going back for a bit more. And then a little bit more.

By the time we finished, there were just a puny few rings of onion left.

We didn't own up.

As for school dinners (for those of us who didn't go home at lunchtime), they may have been mundane, but they were undeniably filling. In the 60s, the norm was a shepherd's pie—a simple yet hearty dish—or as we moved into the 70s, a bland ragu or moussaka (which was nothing like the authentic Greek dish at all) became a staple dish on the school menu.

However, amidst the simplicity, there was a glimmer of excitement in the form of our favourite cherished pudding - a slab of the legendary "chocolate concrete" paired with creamy custard. This chocolate delight possessed a unique character, being firm, dry, and crumbly in texture. Yet, the moment the custard embraced it, the chocolate pudding surrendered its resistance, yielding to its silky touch and transforming into a delectably moist treat. The contrasting sensations of the crispy exterior and the velvety custard created a delicious duet of pleasure in every bite.

On Sunday mornings, the aroma of roast meat would waft from the oven for lunch - it was always a roast dinner on Sundays, without fail.

On warm summer Sunday mornings, my father—with a contented smile on his face—would settle into a chair outside wearing a white string vest and cool Farah trousers, with a steaming mug of tea by his side as the sound of birds chirped in the background created a soothing melody. At the same time, he meticulously scraped a mound of tiny, earthy Jersey Mid potatoes in a bowl of water. They were my father's favourite type of potato, and—although time-consuming to prepare—he enjoyed the chore. His anticipation of eating them with the roast meat was palpable, and we picked up on his sense of joy. Such a simple thing, yet one which brought much family pleasure.

For us 60s children, however, we were overloaded with sweets. We ate them almost every day and lots of them. We could buy several sugary delights for a ha'penny - or more if we could get our hands on a glass pop bottle with a refundable deposit (recycling was a thing even back then). Juicy chews such as Black Jacks, and Fruit Salad, along with sherbet-filled flying saucers or sickly yellow candy bananas and boxes of candy cigarettes. Like most 60's kids, I now have a mouthful of mercury fillings. Visits to the dentist kicked in when I was around ten, and my teeth began to rot. Fillings were a regular dental treatment to be endured as punishment for our sugary pleasures.

Another unhealthy food was a bag of batter bits from the chippy for just a few pennies, although this treat was, thankfully, few and far between since you had to be in the right place at the right time to appropriate such morsels.

And so these foodie smells and tastes belonging to another time and another place remain in the memory, but most of them now are gone, having been replaced by a different diet.

"Here comes your nineteenth nervous breakdoooooowwwn."

It was Saturday morning again, and my father was singing another one of his favourite songs that tickled him pink, 'Here it comes, here it comes, here it comes, here comes your nineteenth nervous breakdown.' He loved this quirky song by the Rolling Stones and sang it lustily as he chopped carrots and onions for his oxtail stew.

Oxtail was a cheap cut of meat, but it was his favourite for stew because of the bones and the gorgeous jelly it produced when it cooled. He cooked it slowly over many hours so that it simmered in its own bone broth, which was rich in collagen. He thickened it with pearl barley and found the leftover stew even more tasty when reheated than it was when it was fresh.

Slurping, sucking sounds would come from my father as he picked his oxtail bones clean. The gristly tops of the oxtail bones came off and inside was succulent marrow to be sucked out. My father had all his own choppers, sharp as a razor, and by the time he'd finished, not a scrap of meat could be found on the bones anywhere - whether they were oxtail, trotters, lamb chops, pork chops, or pork belly ribs, you name it, he'd pick them all dry and got enormous delight from it.

These basic foods sustained and nourished us, and while lacking in the more sophisticated flavours of later decades, they were filling and enjoyed as a family all together around the dinner table.

But it was during the late 60s we realised how fortunate we were compared to other parts of the world. Heartbreaking scenes entered our home through our television screen as we witnessed the sight of Biafran children with swollen bellies and bony limbs - their starvation caused by the Nigerian Civil War in 1967. The distressing scenes form a dark shadow in the memory, for we were powerless to help them. If we could have shared our food, we would have done so willingly.

15. LUXURIES AND HOLIDAYS

I was flying through the air like Mary Poppins, higher and higher.

My parents had taken me to see the (1965) *Mary Poppins* film and I was determined to fly.

Just like her.

So with my mother on my left and father on my right, they lifted me high into the air.

I'd been so engrossed in the film that I was still living the fantasy many days later. I wanted to BE Mary Poppins and I wanted to fly, just like she did, with an umbrella.

But it was not to be in reality. I could only pretend.

Then, just as determined, I wanted to say, 'SUPERCALIFRAGILISTICEXPIALIDOCIOUS'.

But at the age of six, it was a long word to say.

'Superfragalocious. Superfragacal. Supercalifraladosious...' I got so vexed and annoyed with myself for not being able to say the word that I went and shut myself in the toilet.

Silently, then whisperingly, I mastered the long word.

I came out of that toilet, stood in the middle of the living room, and said in a loud voice,

'Supercalifragalisticexpialydocious,' much to the amazement and praise of my parents.

Trips to the cinema (or "darkened houses licensed to show moving pictures" as someone once called them. Why use one word, when you can use seven?) were a luxury and a rare event.

It would be three more years before I set foot in a cinema again when I went to see the film *Oliver!* as an honoured guest of a birthday group.

It would be several years later when I would set foot in a "darkened house licensed to show moving pictures" once more when I went to see *The Exorcist*—an X-rated horror movie—with

Norma. I wasn't quite old enough to see an X-rated film, but I got away with it. Part of the fun was watching a film I wasn't allowed to, and after we'd watched the corny "B" film, we queued up for a slightly melting ice cream from one of the usherettes with trays around their necks. Then we settled back to be scared out of our lives, though we found the film more comical than frightening.

My family very rarely ate out. It was something we didn't do, particularly in the 60s, not even for birthdays. I do not ever recall my parents ever celebrating their birthday or wedding anniversary. I only ever had one birthday party when I was five, where several school friends came to my home, and we played "pass the parcel" amongst other games. Poor Norma ate too much jelly and blancmange and was sick, but generally, celebrating birthdays each year wasn't high on our recreational agenda in the 60s—though as time progressed into the late 80s, special occasions became something to look forward to and an excuse to eat out.

On a couple of occasions, my Aunt Ann would invite me to have a meal at her pub as a special treat, such as on my 16th birthday when I was allowed to invite three friends. And so me, Norma, my little sis and my cousin Vera, sat down and chose a three-course meal from a menu. Vera has never forgotten this occasion, and it demonstrates how simple pleasures that today are quite commonplace meant such a lot in the days when meals out in a restaurant were a rare luxury.

We never even bought cups of tea or coffee when out shopping. Coffee shops were few and far between back in the 60s. Why waste money on buying a cuppa in a shop when you can make one at home for next to nothing, was the unspoken rule.

The only time we would have a drink out was at the pub. My father always enjoyed a pint or two with his family on summer Saturday evenings. The Black Horse pub in Northfield was a favourite venue. We'd go into the gardens at the back and watch the older folk play bowls in their whites while my mother sipped half a lager and lime, my father downed a couple of pints, and I'd be treated to a lemonade and bag of crisps.

It was only as we moved into the 80s that eating out as a family would creep into our lives as something that we were entitled to enjoy. Scampi and chips in a basket was a favourite item my father liked to treat us to, or if it was lunchtime, a cheese and onion sandwich would be ordered with a pint, as public houses started to branch out and expand their business by serving food.

As time went on and my parents got to their forties, they would often go dancing at the local British Legion club. They couldn't do ballroom dancing, but they were excellent at doing the jive, and their movements were seamless as my father expertly led my mother into twirls and spins.

We rarely went on holiday. My father—having been in the Royal Navy—had seen a lot of the world and he was not interested in holiday destinations in Britain whatsoever. He found them utterly boring, but for his family's sake, he made the effort when he could save enough to take us away. I saw the sea for the first time aged five when we went to Great Yarmouth.

First trip to the sea
Great Yarmouth 1965

…on the beer already!

On the pier.
I loved that dress with penguins on, along with my lovely
new soft white Clarks leather summer sandals.

Our next family holiday was 1970 on the Isle of Wight. Crossing over the Solent on the hovercraft felt like we were going abroad. We stayed in a boarding house right on the seafront at Sandown, the back gate opening straight onto the beach. My sister, age two, did not want her photo taken.

Isle of Wight 1970
Little sis, aged 2, refusing to have her photo taken

We never knew when the next holiday would come as it wasn't an annual event.

We never stayed in hotels. They were not only too expensive but also too pretentious for my father's taste due to his sparse upbringing. He preferred a more basic venue. My mother always booked a small boarding house that provided breakfast and a home-cooked evening meal.

An occasional ice cream and a carton of cockles (and gristly whelks for my father) with lashings of salt, pepper and vinegar, were not beyond his means while we were on holiday.

My mother never went abroad once during her 82 years of life, but at the age of 13, I had my first trip abroad when I accompanied my father to Belgium in August 1972.

We travelled by train from Birmingham to get the ferry from Dover to Ostend, and then onward by train to Mons. The reason for this adventure was that my cousin Ronnie (who was much older than me) was in the Royal Navy and based at S.H.A.P.E. (Supreme Headquarters Allied Powers Europe). Ronnie was my Aunt Ann's only son, and he invited my father to visit him there. It was decided I would go too, while my mother and sister remained at home. My parents were very fond of Ronnie, who would often come home from his travels to the Far East with gifts of love: a beautiful red and gold silk Kimono set and a delicate pair of exquisite ornaments depicting life in China stand out in my memory.

My father and I stayed with my cousin Ronnie, his wife and two daughters in their lovely, spacious flat on the S.H.A.P.E. complex in the picturesque village of Casteau, near Mons in Belgium.

My father was a passionate history lover and he eagerly arranged a visit to *Breendonk* in Antwerp. This place, once a detention centre used by the Nazis during World War II, left an indelible mark on my memory. As we stepped inside, the grim sight of the dismal dormitories was stark. A heavy mix of mustiness and despair lingered all around. The visit opened my eyes to a harsh new reality.

We rounded off our visit with a light lunch at "Restaurant Breendonk", where I wrote on the back of our bill, *"nice cheerful well-served place to cheer you up after the dreary cold and dark place where innocent prisoners were kept."*

I was fascinated by the handwriting on the restaurant bill - it was unlike anything I had seen back home. In particular, the way of writing the number seven intrigued me as it had a line across its middle. My cousin Ronnie explained that it was to differentiate between a number one and a number seven. Since then, I have formulated my 7's with a line across its middle...just so's I could connect with a little bit of France in a small way.

Breendonk Memorabilia

On a more pleasant note, I soaked up the essence of life on the Continent, awakening my awareness as I discovered the subtle nuances of their customs - from how they presented a glass of tomato juice to the elegant ambience surrounding it. In the UK, a glass of tomato juice is served simply, perhaps with a hint of Worcestershire sauce upon request. But in Belgium, the elegant waiter delivered it in a tall, exquisite glass adorned with a delicate paper doyley beneath. A slice of lemon was perched gracefully on the side, accompanied by delectable seasoning and a dainty stirrer. It was a small yet profound distinction, and I relished every sip.

I also found the on-site supermarket at S.H.A.P.E called the "Bon Marché" (which my father insisted on calling the "Bob Marsh" in his inimitable way) a new shopping experience, browsing the different brands of Belgian goods. It was a notch up from Lipton's in Northfield, that's for sure.

But we never went again.

Our next family holiday was in 1974 to a rather windy Weston-Super-Mare. We often had lunch on the Grand Pier, where a wonderful pianist played. I would stand by the piano and watch his hands seamlessly fly up and down the keys as he made florid and fluent arpeggios, filling the air with his beautiful music. I was smitten by it. Entranced. *What a beautiful thing to do, playing the piano while people dine…*another musical seed sown.

Sisters, sisters…in Weston-Super-Mare, 1974

In 1976, we had a pleasant week at Tenby. I was 17. It was the last family holiday we had altogether, as so often is the case in families with teenage children.

"In and out of the red balloon, marry the farmer's daughter, sleepy heads in the afternoon, callow la, callow la vita…"

The lyrics of Raymond Froggatt's 1968 hit song rang out as they did every Sunday morning. It was a favourite 45 rpm record that my mother played on our radiogram, as it had a record player as well as a radio. Our record collection was tiny, comprising just a couple of LPs by Barbra Streisand, Marty Robbins, and Marches by the Band of the Royal Marines. My very favourite tunes that captivated my ears and mind were "The Shadow of Your Smile" sung by Barbra Streisand, which gave me goosebumps, and the tragic story told in "El Paso" by Marty Robbins with its jaunty rhythms and catchy melody.

The radiogram was a prized feature in our home for a few years, and we all felt we'd gone up in the world, as not only did it play records, but it was also a very smart piece of furniture made of solid teak. Real teak—not a veneer—for a veneer would never do, for my father detested such falsities. We regarded it as a status symbol in a way.

"Callow la vita! Callow la vita!..." We all joined in the chorus —me, my mother and little sis. The record began to sound a bit scratchy as my mother played it so often, but she loved it.

'That's our Raymond singing that,' she'd remind us proudly. 'Our Froggie, he's so talented.'

Raymond Froggatt was my father's nephew (being the son of my father's older sister, Lucy), and my parents had visited him when he was in hospital recovering after having a kidney removed. They were astonished at not only his resilience and recovery from such a challenging illness but also his rise to stardom as a singer/songwriter.

"Callow la, callow la vita!" We'd sing with gusto in unison with Raymond while doing our various pastimes—me with my colouring, and little sis playing with her Tiny Tears doll, dressing it up in hand-knitted clothes which our kindly neighbour, Mrs Mac, had made. The aroma of roast meat wafted around us as our mother prepared the Sunday lunch and our father scraped a pile of his beloved Jersey Mids.

But as the day wore on a mild sense of foreboding hovered as 4 p.m. approached when my mother would get ready to leave for work at the Royal Orthopaedic Hospital.

She worked there as a domestic cleaner from 5 p.m. until 8 p.m. on four nights a week. My father particularly hated these evenings without her. Me and my sister picked up on his gloom, but we navigated her absence by playing games—either together or apart—and we always enjoyed the sandwiches, cake and other treats that she left us. Our mom would return at about 8.45 p.m. It wasn't a long shift, but my father felt it keenly.

The extra money she earned enabled us to enjoy what we considered to be small "luxuries"—foods such as yoghurts and excellent quality meat from a butcher called Squires in Northfield.

I got my first Saturday job when I was 13 at BaByliss hairdressers on the Bristol Road in Northfield. These were the days when hairdressing salons were busy and bustling with clients and stylists, with women sitting under large hair-drying machines, their heads full of curlers. I swept up the hair cuttings, cleaned the perm rollers and made cups of tea, coffee or hot chocolate for staff and clients, and was paid the grand sum of £1. It was a long day, but my earnings gave me the independence to buy a weekly copy of *Jackie* magazine, some toiletries or Miners makeup—a fashionable cosmetics brand sold in the big Woolworths on the Bristol Road in Northfield. It also helped me to buy some trendy clothes: hot pants, platform shoes, and "flower power" garments that were all the rage. I wanted them all.

One Christmas, a few years later, I got a temporary job with the Post Office. I was paid £20 for two weeks' work delivering the Christmas mail. In those days, the post was delivered extraordinarily early through people's letterboxes, and by 8 am everyone had received their morning mail. I had to get up at 2 am, report to work by 3 am to help sort the letters, and then begin the delivery round at 5 am, assisting my designated postman who showed me the ropes and where to deliver. It was a job I thoroughly enjoyed. There was something magical in delivering people's Christmas mail to their homes.

Our black and white television continued to give us all abundant enjoyment and was considered a luxury, certainly by my parents. We watched all the British classic 60s and 70s programmes week in and week out—comedies such as *Til Death Us Do Part*, shows such as the *Black and White Minstrel Show* (now banned), and my favourite children's programme was *Animal Magic*. However, my father wasn't keen on getting a colour TV when they began to circulate in the early 70s - not least because the TV licence was double what it was for a black and white set. I'm sure it wasn't because he couldn't afford it; he just begrudged paying £10 a year rather than £5.

Other luxuries were the spontaneous gifts my father would buy for us, especially if any of us were unwell. Giving gifts was my father's way of showing concern and cheering us up. Those times certainly stand out in my memory, such as when I was struggling to feel better from a flu-type virus on New Year's Day in 1969. He bought me a beautiful bone china perfume spray from Boots in Northfield—a simple object which I cherished for many years until the pump perished and the cheery yellow floral design faded.

When I was 11, my nose got badly sunburnt, breaking out in painful boils all over. I did look a mess. My face was an awful sight, but my father gave me some money to buy a new pair of black mock-croc shoes which made it all seem better. He found it easier to give gifts than to express affection physically, and I was more than happy with that.

There were many such gifts from my father—not only for myself, but also for my mother and sister—as an expression of his love.

A simple weekly treat was buying sweets when I was small, and I'd often accompany my father, my hand in his, to the sweet shop where we would choose our best-loved confectionary delights. Pineapple chunks, pear drops, mint humbugs, and chocolate limes, to name but a few, were favourites for all the family. But I loved the Jujubes—small multicoloured gums, like jewels: red, yellow, green, pink, orange. Fruity and flavoursome. I relished the lime ones.

The purchase of these small luxuries gave my father much satisfaction, for it was something he'd not been able to experience in his own childhood.

"Bewitched, bothered and bewildered, am I..."

It was Saturday morning, and my father was crooning one of his favourite songs as he sat on the toilet. He loved the alliteration in this song and its crazy sentiments. We could hear him as we ate our 'chooky' eggs for breakfast at the red melamine table in the kitchen.

"I'm wild again, beguiled again, a simpering, whimpering child again..." We could hear his dulcet tones through the door as he sang and read The Birmingham Post while he enjoyed doing a "brace and bit" as he called it ("brace and bit" being Cockney rhyming slang for "shit". My father was very fond of quirky Cockney phrases).

Then, a brief moment of silence.

"When they begin the beguine..." he segued to another of his favourite songs, keeping the alliteration of the B's going, perhaps subconsciously inspired by having a "brace and bit" —all the B's. "It brings back a night of tropical splendour..." he crooned.

He'd spend at least half an hour or more sitting on the loo; it was one of his favourite spots. A haven. A place to chill.

Added to his toileting pleasure was soft toilet paper. Gone were the days of the hard, scratchy Izal brand of tissue paper impregnated with disinfectant. Izal was a cheaper alternative, and many thrifty neighbours would still purchase this medicated toilet roll, which gave off a mild antiseptic odour. In the 60s, Izal was a popular brand in public toilets. It was a hard, non-absorbent, uncomfortable toilet roll to use on delicate body parts. But at least no one would want to nick it. My mother bought it occasionally, and we all hated it, though it was better than the newspaper cut up into squares that my father had used as a child.

Izal was good as tracing paper, though, and we children used it to great effect.

Luxuries were simply defined. For the women in our family —my mother, aunts, and nan—it meant smart, well-crafted clothing and reputable brands of make-up, like Max Factor, along with perfume from Estée Lauder, shoes by Clarks, and high-quality branded items for the home that represented luxury. For the men, it consisted of a few pints and a packet of cigarettes, alongside well-made footwear and clothing that sufficed.

16. SILVER BLADES AND RECREATION

"Inky pinky parlez-vous!"

My father was at it again, singing one of his favourite nonsense songs (thankfully without the extremely rude words).

"There was an old woman of 92, parlez-vous, there was an old woman of 92, parlez-vous, there was an old woman of 92, she always made some rabbit stew, inky pinky parlez-vous!" he yodelled as he polished his shoes. The smell of shoe polish blended with the smell of Daz washing powder as his snotty handkerchiefs were boiling away in the giant old saucepan.

It was Saturday morning in 1970, and he'd begun taking me to Silver Blades Ice Skating Rink in the city centre. We both enjoyed this frequent Saturday morning jaunt, though I was never good at skating. I would queue up to hire a pair of worn, wobbly brown ice skates, and it soon became apparent that they were difficult to skate in. My father bought me a second-hand pair of decent white ones that had more ankle support, enabling me to keep my balance. We couldn't afford lessons—I was too old at the grand old age of 11 anyway—but after a while, I could skate around the rink without falling.

I also learned to skate on one leg with the other up in the air behind me while leaning forward, eyes down looking at the ice, arms out each side like an eagle. On one occasion as I performed this ridiculous manoeuvre, the world around me blurred whilst I focused on maintaining my balance.

Suddenly, disaster struck. My balance faltered and I tumbled to the ice, just as another skater unwittingly glided over the fingers of my right hand. Somewhat shocked, I braced myself for the aftermath.

To my amazement, the damage was minimal. The skater

hurried back to my side, his face etched with concern. Together, we examined my hand, finding only a few shallow scratches from the edge of his blade. His skate must have sliced over the top as there was barely any wound at all - a minor miracle and a fortunate escape from a potentially disastrous injury.

My father loved it best when the rink was occasionally cleared for John Curry (before he became famous). Everyone had to get off the ice and make way for John to have the rink to himself for half an hour.

'He'll go far,' my father prophesied. 'He's top-notch, he is. What a talent,' was his verdict as the young John Curry glided gracefully over the ice.

A fruit bun and a milkshake in the cafe upstairs rounded off a pleasant morning. In the cafe, a giant photo of a skater doing the splits in the air transfixed me. Crikey, how on earth do you do the splits like that from a jump off the ice? I couldn't even do the splits on the ground, let alone jump high enough to do them in mid-flight with a pair of heavy skates on.

By the age of 11 or 12, I was also attending weekly ballet, tap and acro (Acrobatic Arts) classes at a dancing school in Northfield, but I was too old to make any real progress. My body lacked the suppleness needed to do the backbends and other contortions required for the acro classes, and the ballet and tap demanded too much coordination. I never entered any dance exams - I wasn't good enough.

But I vividly remember starring in a mesmerising show that the dancing school laid on at the Birmingham Hippodrome Theatre one year. At our weekly classes, the air was filled with anticipation as we all meticulously rehearsed and prepared for many months, immersing ourselves in the enchantment of the upcoming performance. Our parents, with their skilled hands, crafted exquisite costumes that were a feast for the eyes.

In the show, my beginner's ballet class was transformed into young Hawaiian girls adorned in grass skirts that rustled with every movement. We proudly wore a garland of colourful crêpe paper blossoms around our necks, and together, we harmoniously sang and danced Hawaiian style to the melodious tune of "Yellow Bird up High in Banana Tree", with our voices echoing through the vibrant hall.

Then a quick change of costume ready for our tap routine as mini Fred Astaires.

Amidst the backstage chaos, my senses were overwhelmed by the heady mix of sounds and scents that permeated the atmosphere. The bustling energy of the performers and crew, the echo of footsteps on the wooden floor, intermingled with the occasional laughter and whispered conversations. The aroma of powdered makeup, mixed with the faint hint of sweat, added to the intoxicating ambience.

In that moment, I was captivated by the allure of the stage, enticed by the flurry of excitement that surrounded me. It was a whole new world, brimming with endless possibilities and a sense of exhilaration. If I had possessed the natural talent for dancing, I believe I would have been irresistibly drawn into a captivating stage career.

"Weeeee'll drink, a drink, a drink to Lily the Pink, the Pink, the Pink…"

It was another Saturday morning, and my father, washing his mussels in the kitchen, was in full flow, singing yet another of his quirky songs. This one literally tickled him pink, singing about how Lily the Pink had saved the human race with her "medicinal compound". He loved it. It was one of those bonkers ditties that filled him with glee.

In the living room, little sis was doing a jigsaw, and I was eating a packet of Spangles (picking out all the strawberry ones as they were my favourite) and playing with my Etch-a-Sketch. It's beyond me now why I even liked that toy - it would drive me nuts if I tried to use one today.

My mother had popped up the road to Flowerdew's Fishmongers and Grocers on the Bristol Road for some fresh fish.

When she got home, she untied her headscarf, put the kettle on for our Bird's Mellow coffee, and the radiogram kicked into life, ready for our weekly recreational march around the room to the Band of the Royal Marines.

Oh, such simple pleasures!

Scrinch-scrunch, scrinch-scrunch, scrinch-scrunch…the vivid sound of a thousand marching soldiers as Norma played back her tape recorder was astounding.

We looked at each other, then both fell about laughing until our guts ached.

The reason for the hilarity was the fact that it wasn't a thousand soldiers marching at all, but rather a sound effect Norma had created by the clever use of the microphone on her tape recorder.

We were in her bedroom experimenting with this amazing piece of new technology and recording a play that we'd written and scripted. Our play involved soldiers marching, but how could we recreate the sound of a thousand marching feet?

Norma had had a brainwave; she'd shaved her legs a few days previously, and so she decided to rub the microphone up and down the bristles on one of her legs, in marching time.

We couldn't believe it.

The sound effect she'd created was so realistic it had initially stunned us into silence. Then laughter burst forth as it hit us how she'd achieved this amazing feat. Who'd have thought that scraping a microphone up and down shaved legs would have been so incredibly effective? …BBC eat your heart out.

The tape recorder gave us untold hours of pleasure, mirth and amusement, far more than any of today's devices could.

'C'mon Sunny lads!'

My mother shouted encouragingly at the television.

Second-class division Sunderland was playing football against first-class division Leeds.

''Ark at 'er!' my father said with a smile, delighted that his wife was so excited about a football match.

It was May 1973, and it was the FA Cup final.

My parents wanted the underdogs—Sunderland—to win. Looking back, it was a sort of unwritten thing: championing the underdogs was empowering.

'C'mon Sunny lads, you can do it!' she exclaimed jubilantly.

It was this match, more than the World Cup Finals, that remains vivid in my memory. We were never that interested in football apart from my father, who might tune into Grandstand on a Saturday afternoon, though he much preferred to watch cricket - especially a good test match.

My mother was only interested in football when she "studied" the football pools (yes, "studied" them, I kid you not). It was her chief source of personal recreation to "do the pools" each week. The football pools, or "the pools," is a betting system where participants predict the results of upcoming association football matches.

Neither of my parents were gamblers, but my mother enjoyed putting a few shillings on the pools each week, and my father would bet a few shillings each year on the Grand National.

A man from Vernons' Pools would call each week to collect the completed coupons—along with the "man from the Pru"—my mother was a lifelong believer in insurance with the Prudential.

The pools coupons back then were a myriad of complicated boxes and columns.

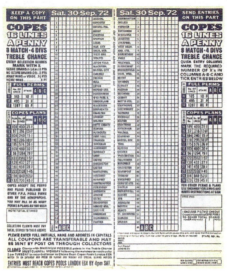

Pools coupon

She was convinced that she could detect patterns and sequences, grappling with the perms, treble chances and divisions and other intricacies on the coupons, confident that there was a formula for a big win. She had a box full of the "keep this part" of pools coupons going back years, and she enjoyed analysing them.

But that big win on the pools never came.

She wasn't a fan of watching football, despite her fascination with the pools, but this FA Cup Final match had us all on the edge of our seats. We all wanted Sunderland to win.

And win they did, against all the odds.

1-0.

The underdogs were the victors.

We were chuffed to bits.

Communal recreation in the neighbourhood came at Christmas, but a major one-off event was the Queen's Silver Jubilee in 1977.

In June of that year, the Jubilee celebrations transformed Wasdale Road into a sensory extravaganza. There was a unity of heart and purpose in planning, organising and contributing to a street party on the big day.

Our street had permission from the council to be officially cordoned off, and the sight of tables, chairs and bunting stretching down the middle of the road created a vibrant scene.

The air was filled with the enticing aromas of party food wafting from the countless plates and bowls. Laughter and joyful chatter mingled with the sounds of children's gleeful shouts and squeals as they participated in lively games and a fancy dress competition.

Union Jacks fluttered in the breeze, adding a colourful touch to the scene. In this moment, laughter and songs filled the atmosphere as the community came together, forming deeper bonds of neighbourly connection.

We belonged to each other.

Jubilee celebrations in Wasdale Road, 1977
Mrs Hamilton waving the flags.

Children enjoying the festivities

Fancy dress competition - they were all winners

(For more historic photos from Wasdale Road Silver Jubilee celebrations, visit Dawn Fallon - Author Blog)

For Norma and me, our friendship remained unshakable as we journeyed into adulthood, revelling in recreational trips both in Birmingham and its leafy surrounding areas in her vibrant yellow Ford. The fact that Norma owned a car and could drive was a fantastic boon. One such special treat was attending a party on the other side of town. We would never have been able to go had it not been for her automobile, particularly as the party was a late-night event, scheduled to go on into the early hours of the morning.

Norma was a typist in the Civil Service, and one of the girls in the typing pool had invited her to a house party—a rare event for us.

However, this particular soirée held a special allure that surpassed any other, for it was a Rasta party nestled several miles away in Handsworth, and we were very excited about it.

Our senses were captivated by the prospect of encountering the vibrant world of West Indian culture. The vivacious warmth of the welcoming West Indian women and the sight of Rastafarian men crowned with their majestic dreadlocks and adorned in resplendent, multicoloured headgear was a special experience. Added to that, the tantalising aroma of exquisite, mouthwatering West Indian cuisine filled the air, enticing us to indulge in its flavoursome delights. And as the night unfolded, we joyfully grooved to the hypnotic pulsating off-beat rhythms of Reggae music into the early hours of the morning...unless we found ourselves nestled beneath the staircase, blissfully devouring the delectable West Indian fare.

It was a jewel of an experience we never forgot.

'Good morning, good mor-or-or-ning! We'll sing the whole day through, good morning, good morning to you!'

This time, it was my mother yodelling at the top of her voice, singing one of her favourite 1950s ditties as we all got ready to have a day out up the Lickey Hills.

Days out were a cheap form of recreation, and a trip to the Lickey Hills was our go-to place for a picnic, where we would romp over the bracken, taking in the picturesque sights with lush greenery and rolling landscapes. The sound of birds chirping and leaves rustling in the gentle breeze would serenade us along the way. We'd finish up in the Old Hare and Hounds pub which had grounds for children to play in while our parents enjoyed a refreshing drink.

Sometimes, as a teenager, I would venture onto the Lickey Hills alone, feeling a sense of liberation in the vastness of nature. During the warm month of August, the air would be filled with the sweet aroma of ripe, plump bilberries. With my hands stained a beautiful shade of purple from picking these juicy delights, I would excitedly gather them to take home and make a mouthwatering bilberry pie, the scent of the berries wafting through the kitchen as it baked.

The Lickey Hills remained a firm favourite, and even when our parents no longer fancied a trip there, me and little sis would go and meet with our Uncle Roy and our cousin Vera for a romp over the hills.

Up the Lickeys with Uncle Roy, cousin Vera and little sis, circa 1974

Occasional trips to Northfield swimming baths were another recreational pastime, particularly for me and Norma, though sometimes my mother would come and enjoy a swim with us. We'd round it off with a bag of steaming hot chips eaten out of newspaper.

Cannon Hill Park was another favourite place for a trip out - particularly to the annual fairground, which my father took me to when I was small. Huge pink and white candy floss balancing on a weedy wooden stick was a sugary mass I enjoyed, despite the knowledge that it would surely contribute to my tooth decay. Its sickly-sweet smell permeated the air, mingling with the fairground hubbub, a mishmash of shoutings, merry-go-round music, laughings, music, and popgun shots. We rounded off the evening with a tasty hotdog on a bed of soggy onions, topped with a generous drizzle of tangy tomato ketchup as we paraded our way to the bus stop and home.

Such simple and ordinary scenes from my past form the patchwork of recreational childhood memories.

"You may talk o' gin and beer
When you're quartered safe out 'ere,
An' you're sent to penny-fights an' Aldershot it."

My father was in his element reciting his favourite poem which he knew by heart.

"But when it comes to slaughter
You'll do your work on water,
An' you'll lick the bloomin' boots of 'im that's got it," he said emphatically, wagging his forefinger for dramatic effect.

"Now in Injia's sunny clime,
Where I used to spend my time
A-servin' of 'Er Majesty the Queen,
Of all them blackfaced crew
The finest man I knew
Was our regimental bhisti, Gunga Din,
      He was 'Din! Din! Din!
      'You limpin' lump o' brick-dust, Gunga Din!
      'Hi! Slippy hitherao
      'Water, get it! Panee lao,
      'You squidgy-nosed old idol, Gunga Din.'"

This poem by Rudyard Kipling extolling the faithful service of Gunga Din, an Indian water carrier in the British Army, painted a vivid picture, and with its zingy pulse and rhythmic patterns, it became a firm family favourite. My father particularly loved the last line:

"You're a better man than I am, Gunga Din."

…And we loved it too, waiting in anticipation for it.

I guess it spoke of the underdog being the victor again.

We were enthralled by the tuneful words of the melodic verses and we sat spellbound as he enunciated every syllable.

My father had left school aged fourteen. He'd had a Catholic education as his mother was a practising Catholic and sent all her children to Catholic school. His education had been cut short due to his working-class status and the need for him to find work. But from somewhere—whether it was school or some other source, perhaps the Royal Navy—he had developed a love and appreciation of poetry.

I guess he had an innate love of words. This love of words he imparted to us as children, and he would often recite poems which had tickled his fancy - and they tickled ours too, being frequently recited, they were never forgotten.

Although my father enjoyed reading, we never had many books in our home. He would always borrow books from Northfield Library for himself. Buying books was considered an expensive luxury - why buy books when you can borrow them for free? He preferred non-fiction, and true crime was his favourite genre, as well as submarine warfare. The only book I remember my father buying was a paperback called "Puckoon" by Spike Milligan. When I learned to read, my mother bought me a few Ladybird storybooks. "Tiptoes, The Mischievous Kitten" was my all-time favourite and I read it many times over, relishing the vivid colours in the beautiful illustrations.

"The Owl and the Pussycat" was another favourite verse that dad would recite in full by heart with much conviction despite it being so fanciful. I guess it appealed to him because it is a nonsense poem and slightly bonkers. Its symmetry and vivid descriptions captured our hearts and minds, transporting us to another world with the owl, the pussycat, a pea green boat, honey and money, Bong trees, a Piggy-wig, slices of quince, a runcible spoon and a marriage where they "danced by the light of the moon, the moon, they danced by the light of the moon..." Superb.

Snippets from other poems would be voiced by our dad, such as John Masefield's "Sea Fever" and the evocative line, 'I must go down to the seas again, to the lonely seas and the sky, and all I ask is a tall ship and a star to steer her by,' along with Newbolt's poem "Drakes Drum", where he would misquote it, leaving out a few lines.

"Drake was in his hammock and a thousand miles away, a-dreaming all the time of Plymouth Hoe," he would recite dreamily. Plymouth was where he'd been stationed when he'd served in the Royal Navy. He loved that poem. He loved Plymouth Hoe. It transported him back to a former time and place.

My father even quoted a Shakespeare poem, "Who is Sylvia, what is she..." proclaiming it as if it were a question. He never recited any more than that, but it was enough. Those six words packed a punch in themselves, such was their genius.

And then there was the Robbie Burns poem "To A Louse".

"Ye ugly, creepin, blastit wonner,
Detested, shunn'd by saunt an' sinner,
How daur ye set your fit upon her --
Sae fine a lady!
Gae somewhere else and seek your dinner
On some poor body."

My father would recite several of his favourite lines from memory with passion and such a strong Scottish accent, you'd have thought he'd been born there. He truly enjoyed spitting it out in the Scottish brogue, and his anger at the impudent louse was evident in his delivery of it.

"I wad na been supris'd to spy
Ye on some auld wife's flainen toy..."

He adored the vivid scenes it portrayed, and he delighted in explaining and educating us about the meaning of the poem. Its subject matter tickled him pink. The picture of a fine lady sitting in church with an ugly louse crawling on her was an incongruity he found both fascinating and irresistible.

But it was the final verse with its powerful punch line he loved the best and he delivered with great aplomb,

"O wad some Pow'r the giftie gie us,
To see oursels as ithers see us!"

Such was the power of poems in a working-class home, to bring us all much pleasure and bonding, even if they were slightly misquoted or were not recited in their entirety, they were valued, loved, and they sang to our hearts.

A recreation which cost nothing yet was rich in pleasure.

115

17. COUSINS AND RELLIES

Interactions and experiences with my relatives form a smorgasbord of evocative memories which I cherish.

My parents moved to the south of Birmingham, several miles away from their close relatives who all lived on the opposite side of the city. Since neither of my parents could drive, we relied on public transport to visit family members. It often took two or three bus rides to the other side of town, so visits were generally infrequent. The only exception was my mother's weekly trip to see my grandmother, Doris. I didn't see my aunts or cousins from either side of the family that often.

On my father's side, meetings with his family usually revolved around his sister's pub, The Three Horseshoes, in Sheldon. He would sometimes meet two of his closest brothers, Tom and Billy, for a pint at weekends.

My Uncle Tom had a keen sense of humour and made all his nephews and nieces laugh every time we met him.

I vividly remember when he came to visit us one summer Sunday at Wasdale Road. After several bevvies (drinks) at the Black Horse with my father, he'd had a great nap and then livened himself up with a refreshing swill (cold water splashed on the face). At the time, my mother was pregnant with my little sis (though we had no idea it was a girl). I was riding my three-wheeler bike in the back garden, and he came to chat with me to discuss possible names for the baby. After several suggestions from me, he declared that he thought we should call the newborn "Mudgard".

I don't know why, but it cracked me up.

I guess it was because I found the incongruity of a cute infant being called Mudgard to be an incredibly quirky concept.

Uncle Tom eventually emigrated to Australia as one of the

Ten Pound Poms. He had to borrow most of the money from my father as he didn't have a penny to his name at the time, and word had got around that my father had a bit of cash stashed as he was saving up to buy an expensive Axminster carpet... oooh, my poor mother was not well pleased that she had to wait several more months for that carpet while Uncle Tom paid it back in instalments from down under.

Uncle Tom settled in Melbourne and built a new life for himself. He didn't have any children, and when I was older, in my 20s, I enjoyed writing to him in Australia, learning about his life in Oz and what he'd been up to. Once again, the Smith trait for giving gifts manifested as Tom showered his nieces with random presents: beautiful Australian opal pendants and various items of 9ct gold jewellery would arrive in the post now and again. After his partner Alma died, he moved back to the U.K. as a longing for family ties was strong, and he was drawn back to Birmingham to be near his brothers and blood family.

My Uncle Bill had two children, David and Christina Rosina (fondly called Chrissie by my family), and Billy was one of the brothers closest to my father (who insisted on calling him "Libby"—another of his Spoonerisms). They didn't always see eye to eye and could have some slanging matches, but they loved each other dearly and weren't afraid to show each other physical affection with a warm embrace, with my father telling his younger brother, "I love you, Libby," and Billy responding, "I love you too". A true "Bromance".

Uncle Bill was a character and, like all the Smith brothers, could be quite comical. When they got together, it was a bagful of laughs. The brothers spoke in a strong Birmingham dialect and weren't slow in coming forward with their opinions. But they all had hearts of gold and loved us kiddies to bits, calling us "bab", "babby", or "chick".

Uncle Bill once bought my sister a portable typewriter when she was a teenager—a random act of kindness she never forgot— once again demonstrating that the giving of gifts was a primary love language in the Smith family. Generosity was their way of expressing affection and tenderness towards those they loved and cared for.

Billy was fondly known as "Billy Blue" because he was a staunch supporter of Birmingham City Football Club (their nickname being "The Blues" due to the colour of their football kit). All the Smith brothers were Blues fans, regularly attending home matches at St Andrew's in Birmingham.

Billy visited us one sunny Sunday at Wasdale Road in 1971, bringing his son, Dave, with him. Dave was around the same age as me, and laughter filled the air as we played in the back garden, with the familiar creak of my beloved swing echoing around us as we soared higher and higher, launching ourselves into the air as the swing reached its peak height and landing with a thud on the grass. Dave would go so high I would hold my breath as he reached the pinnacle. I was convinced he was going to loop the loop and go full circle over the top of the swing before swooping back down. He very nearly did.

My mother fussed around us, supplying us with biscuits and Alpine fizzy pop, while our dads went off for a few bevvies at the Traveller's Rest in Northfield. Then, as my mother prepared dinner, the aroma of delicious roast beef wafted from the kitchen, making our stomachs growl.

Dave was starting senior school later that year, and my father gave him a pound note along with some advice, 'Eat humble pie when you're at school, and you'll get on well,' he said. Dave hadn't got a clue what humble pie was; he'd never eaten it before, and he was expecting it to be on the school lunch menu. He got very worried when he couldn't find it. Such is the misunderstanding that can arise between adults and children.

During the 80s Billy had a dog called Blue, a Staffordshire Bull Terrier, and his pedigree name was Baracane Billy The Kid. Unfortunately, Blue had a nasty streak—whether from nature or nurture, it wasn't known. He had longish legs for a Staffie, so he could have been too closely bred, though his brother, Ben, was a prize winner and looked proper Staffie. My father was scared stiff of Blue and steered clear of him. But Billy, Dave and little

Chrissie all got bit.

Family ties and bonds continued long after our childhood. My cousin Dave recalls a very emotional moment shared between him and my father. In December 1982, Dave and his mate spilt out of a pub in high spirits, skylarking around as their laughter and banter echoed through the car park. The air was chilly and filled with the strong scent of alcohol and car exhaust fumes as they got into their cars and revved the engines. Off they zoomed.

Then, without warning, the screeching of tyres and shattering of glass rang in Dave's ears as he crashed into his friend's car, writing it off in the impact. With no seat belt on, he hit his head on the roof of his own vehicle. It was a painful reminder of his foolishness for drinking too much, and he was arrested.

The police station, dimly lit, smelling of urine and stale sweat, became his temporary prison. The sound of heavy metal doors slamming echoed through the cold, sterile hallway as the officers took pleasure in relaying the message of his punishment to his father, Billy.

Dave was released on Christmas Eve, and the atmosphere at home was tense. The flickering lights from the Christmas tree cast a sombre glow as the smell of alcohol lingered in the air. Billy—himself still inebriated from a booze-up the previous night—launched into a lecture to his son Dave, his words blending with the sound of frustration rising, for Dave was not in the mood to be admonished, and a verbal exchange flared up. The room felt suffocating, and the tension escalated until violence erupted. The force of the blows between them sent Dave crashing over the arm of the sofa, a sharp pain shooting through his body.

Then, out of nowhere, the air was filled with growls, snarls and barks from Blue, Billy's Staffordshire Bull Terrier, a menacing presence in the room.

Fear mixed with adrenaline as Blue lunged for Dave's throat, narrowly missing its mark. Blue's teeth sank into him despite his efforts to fight him off. Blood stained the scene, pooling beneath him as wounds from Dave's lip, hand, and foot gushed crimson. The metallic scent of blood mingled with the stench of fear, created a nauseating combination, as Dave was blue-lighted away in an ambulance for treatment. His lip needed 27 stitches.

A week later, my father visited Billy and Dave, and after a New Year's booze-up at the Hare and Hounds, they sauntered back to Billy's house. The weight of depression hung heavy in the air from all the upset, and the living room seemed to absorb the sadness Dave was feeling. Billy went upstairs for a nap, and my father sat beside Dave on the sofa, both of them drunk and smelling of alcohol. Sensing Dave's despondency and heaviness of heart, my father put his arms around him, assuring him everything would turn out all right. The weight of his embrace brought a sense of comfort to Dave, as the warmth of my father's hug offered solace in the room.

My father, too, had known painful times in the past, and then it was Dave's turn to console my father. Tears flowed freely, the sound of their sobs intermingled with the soft tick of the clock on the mantelpiece. In that vulnerable moment, they lit a fag, the scent of smoke clinging to their clothes—a tangible reminder of their shared pain. Through tear-streaked eyes, my father urged Dave to grow a moustache to hide the scar that marred his face, which, in time, he did.

The gravity of those moments etched themselves into Dave's memory, forever intertwined with the sights, sounds, smells, and emotions that accompanied them. Dave still misses my dad to this day, remembering him as someone generous, always getting the beer in. He's never forgotten that my father made a large contribution to his Blues football season ticket on his 50th birthday. The giving of gifts to express affection was always there.

My father's older sister, Ann, was also generous to all her

relatives, particularly her nephews and nieces, and she was wonderfully hospitable and a marvellous hostess, to boot.

I adored visiting my Aunt Ann's pub—The Three Horseshoes in Sheldon—a sensory wonderland that captivated me. The moment I stepped inside, I was drawn to the nooks and crannies that beckoned exploration. The air was filled with the whiff of beer and stale smoke.

As I explored my way through the pub, being free to roam, my aunt's majestic Alsatian, named Shandy, would often shadow me. The sound of his paws echoing on the hard floors resonated throughout the space, adding a lively rhythm to the ambience. And there, nestled in a cosy corner or curled up under the ovens in the kitchen, was Tipsy, my aunt's elegant black cat, emanating an air of mystery.

In the grounds of The Three Horseshoes pub

My parents always dressed well, especially when going out, looking smart.

When I was a baby, Shandy would keep a loyal guard over my pram, a sight that filled my mother with a sense of comfort.

The name Shandy, just like the refreshing drink, seemed fitting for such a regal companion. And Tipsy—a name that danced on the tip of my tongue—seemed perfect for the mischievous feline. We thought that Shandy and Tipsy were cool names for pub pets.

Several years later, we acquired a tabby cat and called her Tipsy, a tribute to the original Tipsy who had graced the pub with her presence.

Our Tipsy

Amidst the lively pub atmosphere, one particular sensory delight stands out in my memory - Shandy's Bonios. These dry and tasteless dog biscuits held an inexplicable allure for me, though I have no idea why. The texture of each bite and the satisfying crunch captivated my young palate. They didn't seem to do me any harm, but I'd be horrified if I saw any child eating a Bonio these days.

My Aunt Ann's pub was more than just a place to enjoy drinks and crisps. It was a sensory haven, a palace of sights, sounds, smells, and tastes that left an indelible impression in my mind.

Of all my father's relatives, we visited Aunt Ann the most. She was a gifted knitter, and for birthdays and Christmas, she would knit me beautiful matching "twin sets" or—as I grew older—she would bestow gifts of money, a trend she maintained until I was 18. She loved being generous on special occasions, and for my tenth birthday she not only invited me and my family for a meal at her pub, but she arranged for a Mr Khan to visit the pub and he had a surprise for me: a beautiful anorak in vivid floral colours was presented to me. These gestures of love brought her much happiness.

She often put on lavish Christmas or New Year parties for her family. It was during the festive season that Aunt Ann truly outdid herself. She transformed her pub into a winter wonderland, twinkling fairy lights illuminating every corner. The sound of laughter and lively conversations echoed through the bar.

One particular year stands out in my memory. Aunt Ann had prepared a grand New Year's Eve party after closing hours. The pub lounge was adorned with colourful decorations, shimmering tinsel, and a magnificent Christmas tree that sparkled with ornaments.

And then, there it was, towering over me like a giant from a fairytale - a colossal cracker, as big as a bolster pillow. Its vibrant colours and shimmering paper captivated my attention, promising hidden treasures within. Aunt Ann's mischievous smile filled the room as she declared that it could only be pulled at midnight.

As a seven-year-old, midnight felt like an eternity away. The anticipation built with every passing minute, the ticking of the clock seemed slow. Finally, the moment arrived, and with several of us joining in for the pull, a resounding crack echoed as the cracker burst open, showering the room with confetti, paper hats, jokes, party blowers, and tiny surprises.

The room erupted with excitement as we eagerly picked through the scattered treasures, marvelling at the small trinkets and sweets nestled within. The joy and wonder on everyone's faces were palpable as if the magic of the holiday season had come alive in that very moment.

So embedded in my mind was the magic of the giant cracker,

thirty-five years later when the new millennium dawned, I decided I'd make my own giant cracker as midnight struck for the year 2000.

Giant cracker I made especially for the year 2000.
I wanted my son - then aged five - to experience the same
sense of wonder with such a vast celebratory item!

Later, Ann and her husband Ron moved to The Billesley pub in Kings Heath. Me and little sis loved going there as the pub was enormous with big cloakrooms and corridors - just perfect for playing Hide and Seek. Ron had a Jaguar, which we thought was dead posh. The scent of its leather and wood interior filled our nostrils if we were ever fortunate enough to be given a lift back home.

On one occasion, when I was about six, the sun beamed down on a serene Sunday afternoon as my parents paid a rare visit to Vinny and Sid. Vinny was my father's youngest sister (Lavinia was her full name). They had two children, Jane and Tony, and they lived a couple of bus rides away.

My cousin Tony—who was around the same age as me—hatched a plan to show me around the local area and explore the streets without alerting anyone to our whereabouts. We left the house without a by-your-leave. As we ventured forth, the bustling sights and sounds of the neighbourhood enveloped us. We revelled in the warmth of the sun on our skin, the state of the front gardens, and the melodic chirping of birds.

We celebrated a newfound sense of freedom.

However, our carefree wanderings led us astray, and panic began to seep in as Tony's memory of how to get back home failed him. The air grew heavy with uncertainty, and the scent of anxiety lingered.

As time passed, our parents noticed our absence, and, consumed by worry, teetered on the edge of contacting the authorities. Just as their desperate thoughts turned to action, Tony's innate sense of direction miraculously kicked in, guiding us back to safety in the nick of time, averting the impending alarm. Their relief at our appearance spared us a scolding. My dad blamed Tony, and his dad blamed me for our illegal escapade. We remained silent partners in crime.

I never got lost again.

The next time I visited Vinny's house was several years later on a beautiful summer morning for Jane's wedding in 1973. I was honoured to be one of her bridesmaids. It was the only time I'd ever been a bridesmaid, and I cherished the experience. I was deeply touched that I'd been chosen for such a privileged role and relished every moment, loving our pale blue dresses, white satin bridal shoes, headbands and our beautiful, tiny Bibles flowing with ribbon…what girl doesn't love being a bridesmaid?

Bridesmaid experience - I am on the right at the end, standing next to my younger cousin, Chrissie, my Uncle Billy's daughter (who my father later nicknamed Mrs Chorington as she was well known for doing many chores around the home).

My mother had two married sisters, Brenda and Ruth, plus a younger brother, Roy—or Royston as he was sometimes called —who was the 'baby' of the family, having been born to my grandparents when they were late in life. At the grand age of three, Roy had become an uncle. He must have been one of the youngest uncles in the country.

My nan lived at 103 Birdbrook Road, Great Barr, and all the siblings met there as often as they could for a get-together. My grandfather, Tom, had died in 1963, so my nan was a widow and her son, Roy, lived with her.

My maternal grandmother (nan), Doris, and my mother. Circa 1956. In the back garden at 103 Birdbrook Road.

A few doors down stood a grocery store that sold delicious

best ham, where we'd be sent with a shopping list to buy victuals for afternoon tea.

The tantalising aroma of the cured meat wafted through the air, tickling the senses of anyone who ventured near. Inside, the grocer stood behind the counter, his skilled hands effortlessly operating the electric meat slicer. The rhythmic hum of the machine harmonised with the soft clink of metal against metal, creating a symphony of slicing. Mesmerised, I watched as the ham transformed into thin, juicy slices, ready to grace our sandwiches.

Alongside the ham, we bought loaves of my grandmother's favourite brand of bread—Slimcea or Nimble—along with some best butter. Then, a tin of salmon, some fresh salad, and a decadent Victoria sponge with its sweet aroma completed our purchase, along with a "ka-ching" from the old cash till. With our bounty in hand, we returned to my grandmother's back room, where the comforting warmth of a cuppa awaited us. There, the familiar sights, sounds, and smells surrounded us along with the love of the family. We savoured the exquisite simplicity of sandwiches filled with juicy ham and a smattering of English mustard, or sandwiches filled with briny tinned salmon mashed to a pulp in vinegar, making the thin Slimcea bread moist and almost soggy.

My grandmother's house always had a cosy and familiar ambience. The moment I stepped inside, the sight of her cherished mismatched trinkets and ornaments adorned every corner, creating a visually captivating atmosphere. It also had a distinctive whiff of familiar smells - that of pungent ripening fruit in the bowl, Mr Sheen spray polish, fragrant Max Factor face powder and her beloved Estée Lauder Youth Dew perfume: all these mingled into one pong which would linger in the nostrils long after I'd left…except for the time when my little sis did the polishing, as she often did, and was beavering away with spray can in hand, spraying all the surfaces liberally.

'Oh darling,' said our nan in her posh voice—a voice that both she and my mother often adopted, 'what a lovely smell that is compared to the usual one,' she observed, noticing a difference in aroma.

Little sis was a bit puzzled. So she looked at the can. She'd been using fly killer instead of polish. *Crikey, she could have killed more than just the flies! No wonder the budgie had gone quiet.* Mind you, polishing and other household chores should have been done by a visiting home help, but it seemed our nan preferred her to just sit down and listen rather than do any real work. But then, if that's what our nan wanted, I guess the home help was a great help, though not in her officially employed capacity!

The room at the front of the house was never lived in, and it emitted a subtle musty aroma, intensified during the winter months when the cold, damp air seeped through the unheated space. An upright piano stood against a wall, its slightly yellowing keys inviting to the touch. My nan couldn't read music, but she could 'vamp' (as my mother called it) and occasionally she'd sit and play "You Made Me Love You" singing along with the words, 'I didn't want to do it, I didn't want to do it,' she'd trill as her right hand played the tune and her left hand swooped across the lower keys vamping a bass note before hitting a relevant chord.

A display cabinet showcased an assortment of knick-knacks, catching the light and casting delicate shadows, whilst a large, dark red settee in a coarse bouclé fabric filled the centre of the room. My grandmother loved all her trinkets and trimmings, and her home was peppered with various ornamental objects.

At the back of the house, the small, cluttered living room was connected to a minuscule kitchen with an even more minuscule pantry. The living room, with a constant backdrop of noisy chirruping chatter from the budgerigar, overflowed with an assortment of furniture, from the folding drop leaf table under the window where meals were shared to the television that provided endless entertainment.

However, the true heart of the room was my grandmother's cherished armchair, positioned proudly in the centre. Its faded fabric and worn antimacassars on the armrests told stories of countless hours of comfort and companionship. The fire was on, come summer and winter, along with the television.

My grandmother loved her telephone, and she told us that she would often ring the Samaritans for a chat. We weren't overly concerned that she was suicidal, but after we all went home, loneliness could surface, and she enjoyed a natter to a listening ear on the end of the blower.

On the wall, a photo hung of my nan's daughter, Greta, who died at the age of 7 from peritonitis. The loss of Greta must have been a sadness my nan carried with her to her dying day. She and my mother often spoke fondly of "our Greta"—not with bitterness or melancholy—but with fond remembrance of a beautiful little girl whose life was cut short.

Greta
I always thought I looked a little like her when I was her age

She had also lost her firstborn son, John, who died when he was around 18 months old - a traumatic bereavement that was never spoken about, yet a loss that parents carry in their heart for a lifetime.

Next to Greta's photo was a proper cuckoo clock, and I loved it. The cuckoo came out on the hour, every hour, and I was mesmerised by the little bird peepo-ing, along with the realistic cones that swung on chains underneath.

Stepping outside the back door from the tiny kitchen, a musty, dusty coal house stood, its presence filled with intrigue and mystery to a young child. The darkness within seemed to hold secrets waiting to be discovered, evoking a sense of wonder and curiosity.

Beyond the coal house, a rambling garden sprawled out. The crowning jewel of the garden was a magnificent apple tree, reaching towards the sky with branches that seemed to stretch endlessly. In the autumn, apples galore would drop to the ground, creating quite a mess. The tree was a superb climbing frame, beckoning daring climbing expeditions, offering a vantage point to survey the world from above. How none of us ever fell and broke any bones is a minor miracle.

For many years, a dog called Pepe (a rather posh spelling for a name pronounced "Peppy") graced my nan's home and bounded around the back garden. She was a black-with-a-bit-of-white-cross-collie-type of dog. No one quite knew where she came from, but Roy would often take her for a walk around the local gullies. Of this dog, my father knew very little, otherwise she may have been called "Pepe-Poo-Pah". Nevertheless, Roy bestowed upon her the grand name of "Pepe-Puppy, Doggy-Woggy, Pally-Sally, Lassie Davies, Wuff, Wuff, Wuff." I am sure my father would have wholeheartedly approved of such nomenclature.

Roy also had four fancy mice in a wooden box in his bedroom for a while, with equally fancy names, considering they were rodents: Wright, Mason, Waters, and Barrett. Of course, anyone familiar with Pink Floyd will know that those fancy names are the surnames of the four members of the group. But unknowingly, Roy had misgendered at least one of the mice as they started breeding. Proliferously. So they had to go.

My nan's mobility was poor when I was small, and unfortunately, she became more disabled as the years went by and developed very bad feet. Her ankles collapsed and her feet were badly swollen. Eventually, she had to use a wheelchair and sleep downstairs, with a commode in the living room. She became housebound and cherished our visits and company even more.

Each time we visited I would brush her hair for a long time, and curl it with her curling irons. Then she'd love for me to put some makeup on her face. The buttery-velvety scent of Crème Simon M.A.T. face cream filled the air while I moisturised her skin before applying Max Factor face powder, finally adding the finishing touches of Max Factor cake mascara (the sort we spat into to moisten and then applied with a small brush). Then a dash of lipstick completed the look. However, it was the small, round cardboard box of rouge I loved the best as I gave her cheeks a flush of colour.

As my sister grew, she carried on the role of being a hairdresser and make-up artist.

My nan didn't have much money, but she would always buy nice clothes and decent brands of make-up and perfume. It cheered her up, expressed her individuality and helped her well-being. She relished the attention when we combed her hair and applied her make-up and she found the pampering soothing, making her feel special and loved.

As time passed, a bright light entered her life when she met the elegant and cultured Bernard, who brought companionship and interest into her world. He was knowledgeable about music, antiques and all kinds of subjects.

It's uncertain how Doris (my nan) and Bernard met— possibly at a weekly club where Doris would be picked up and dropped back home afterwards, as she was so bad on her feet.

Bernard used to go to the club with his wife Kath, but then continued going to the club to meet up with friends after he became a widower. He would visit Doris in the early evening on most days and at lunchtime on weekends. He eventually chose to give up his home, which was only a mile or so away and went to live with Doris and Roy.

My uncle Roy was more like a cousin because he was only a few years older than me and my other cousins.

As we grew, Roy's sharp wit and somewhat maverick outlook on life made him fun to be with, and he was always skylarking around, making us laugh or entertaining us with his music. I particularly liked his rendering of "A Whiter Shade of Pale". He could play the piano, organ and guitar - Pink Floyd was a firm favourite in my nan's front room where all the music happened.

In the mid-70s, Bernard became terminally ill, with nuns attending him in Birdbrook Road. It was young Roy who walked the two miles to Bernard's son's house to inform his family that they should visit. Bernard's granddaughter, Bernadette— or Bunny as she is fondly called—answered the door. It was a pivotal moment for the two families, for Bunny and Roy were soon married, and our families were forever intertwined.

Bernard would have been well pleased.

My aunt Brenda was my nan's eldest daughter. Brenda and her husband, Mike, were childless, so she was particularly happy to have me over to their home for sleepovers. She took all her nephews and nieces under her wing and loved nothing more than to spoil us all.

She would buy me "Lucky Bags" every time I visited, along with colouring books and crayons - such simple things to give a child, yet ones which brought a smile to our faces and made us feel loved and special.

Brenda's exuberant sense of humour filled the air with echoing laughter and playful merriment, creating a vibrant atmosphere at every family gathering. Her jokes had everyone doubled over in stitches, their joyful tittering reverberating through the room.

She would play tricks and practical jokes on everyone, and we never knew who would be next in line for one of her pranks. My little sis was at the end of one such frolic when Brenda squirted her with washing-up liquid, only to find it was a piece of string that had shot out of the bottle.

We all knew Brenda had a soft spot for Tom Jones; it was evident in the way her eyes sparkled whenever his name was mentioned or if he came on the television gyrating his hips. With a mischievous twinkle, she would playfully tease and make mild sexual innuendos, adding a touch of flirtatious charm to the occasion.

The sleepovers at Brenda's house at 54 Heathfield Road in Handsworth during the 60s were a sensory delight. The old villas stood tall with four storeys, the weathered walls holding stories of the past. It was a big, big house. Cellar at the bottom. Three rooms plus a kitchen and a large veranda with a loo on the ground floor. Three bedrooms and a toilet with a separate bathroom on the first floor. Then another staircase up to the attic.

As I entered her house, a musty scent of history and nostalgia greeted me, blending with the faint aroma of wood polish. The creaking of the wooden floorboards beneath our feet echoed through the rooms, whispering secrets of the past.

The attic beckoned with its mysterious allure, its dimly lit space filled with the scent of old books, dust and mysterious objects. I would climb the stairs, my fingers grazing the rough texture of the wooden bannister, as I ventured into a world of wonder and curiosity, ready to explore the boxes stashed away... and to the train set and station with a homemade papier-mâché landscape and tunnel. Everything an attic should be.

The cellar, hidden beneath the ground, held its own secrets. The musty smell intensified as I descended the stone steps, the cool air sending a shiver down my spine. In the dim light, my fingers brushed against forgotten relics, the touch of history tingling my senses. It was a place where the imagination ran wild, where every object held a story waiting to be discovered. A tad spooky, it wasn't my most favourite place to be, but one which had to be visited.

The only thing I couldn't get used to was the *vroom vroom*

vroom of cars at night passing by my bedroom at the front of the house on the main road, which would keep me awake. I was so used to living on a quiet road at home, my ears found it difficult to block out the traffic sounds.

Brenda's house in Handsworth was more than just a physical space; it was a haven of sights, sounds, smells, and feelings. It was a place where laughter echoed, where the scent of history lingered. Who had lived in these once elegant villas before? What stories could the walls tell?

Brenda and Mike had a Corgi called Sherry, and I was fascinated by this breed of affectionate dog. I can understand why the Queen liked them. But there was a golden rule: every time I stroked Sherry, I had to go and wash my hands afterwards. It was a ritual played over and over, for I stroked the dog many times.

Brenda and Mike were a little more affluent than the rest of the family. Mike worked at Hamstead Colliery until it closed in 1965, then found work in a factory, and Brenda, being good with numbers, worked full time, loving her job in the accounts office at Lewis's, a big department store in the city centre. We would occasionally visit her there, watching her at work with a bright orange rubber finger tip flicking through papers, collating and counting numbers, then we'd have lunch together in the staff canteen.

Brenda and Mike were the only relatives on my mother's side with a car at that time. They had a mustard-coloured Maxi, which I thought was top-notch.Day trips to Cheddar Gorge, Minehead and the Lickey Hills in the trendy Maxi were frequent highlights.

Eventually, they moved to a more modern house at 39 Yateley Avenue in Great Barr, and Brenda was the first in the family to have a large freezer in her kitchen. She kept frozen meat and veg in it and—shock horror—bread! My parents were puzzled by this phenomenon.

Freezing bread?

It was unheard of.

We never quite believed that bread could taste good after being frozen. I don't know why. It was many years before I did it myself and found out that freezing bread is great.

Often at Christmas, Brenda would have us all round to her house where she'd put on a marvellous spread of food, including her delicious lemon meringue pie, along with little presents for us children, and the bingo game would come out. The jokes, laughter, and mildly naughty innuendos often resulted in raucous laughter. Brenda was the life and soul of the party.

Visits to my Aunt Ruth and four cousins in Walsall were a whole different level of experience for an only child like myself (until my little sis came along), and I cherished spending time with them. They lived in Glastonbury Crescent on the Mossley Estate in Bloxwich. It was a long journey on public transport from where we lived in Northfield to the Mossley Estate, but worth it.

Ruth was married to Mick, who was from Yugoslavia, and they had four children who were bestowed with Slavic names. The boys were Ljuba (Ljubomir), Tommy (Tomislav), and Nicky (Nikola), with Vera being the only girl. I loved their Yugoslavian names, and Mick gave Ruth the Slavic name of "Radmilla". I thought they all sounded very exotic.

As an only child for eight years, it was a bit of a culture shock for me to experience a larger family. Life was full on when I visited them.

My Aunt Ruth was an exuberant, generous person and full of life. Her front door was always open and never locked, with random neighbours popping in throughout the day for a cuppa and a natter. As Christmas approached, she'd sit on the living room floor, with her legs splayed out, peeling a pile of onions to pickle, for sharing.

We all called Mick (Mirko was his Slavic name) Chicka Mick, and I have a vivid memory that he never wore slippers; he much preferred padding around the house in his socks. I loved his accent. He spoke very good English indeed, but he always got saucers and saucepans mixed up. Added to that, he always poured his hot tea into his saucer and slurped it, as the tea cooled quicker in the saucer (which he called a saucepan) because he couldn't wait for it to cool in the cup.

He worked for a while as a miner at Hamstead Colliery.

'If we see the canary fall, we have to get out quick!' he used to say.

I thought he was joking. A canary? Down a coal mine? Yet it is indeed true that canaries were used down the mines until 1986. With their unique breathing habits, the canaries would quickly show symptoms of carbon monoxide poisoning and other toxic gases, alerting the men to danger, giving them more time to evacuate.

A bonus of working down the mine was the free coal they had before all the council properties changed over to gas. The mine closed in 1965—the end of an era—and Chicka Mick then went to work for IMI in Stafford.

Mick was born in 1925 in Bratunac - a small, picturesque village nestled in the verdant Baltic hills. He left his home and family at the tender age of 16 after fighting against his country and the communists, building a new life and family for himself in England with my Aunty Ruth.

My Aunt Ruth was an amazingly resilient person, and in the late 1960s, she took her four children to visit their paternal grandmother and other relatives in Bratunac, Yugoslavia. Their grandfather had passed away during the war.

Mick could not travel with them as tensions in the country prevented him from travelling there safely - he would have been arrested.

'Chicka Mick can't go with them!' my mother bewailed at the thought of her sister travelling nearly 1500 miles by sea and train with four children aged eleven and under to Bratunac, 'he said he'd be shot if he returned there!'

We were all amazed that Ruth had the unflinching motivation to go through with her plan, and go through with it she did.

Undaunted by the distance and logistics of such a journey, she set off with young Ljuba, aged eleven, Tommy, aged nine, Vera, aged eight and young Nicky, aged just five, in tow. She was determined her children would meet their paternal relatives - to honour Mick's family, and also as an important part of the children's identity and family ties.

It was an adventure, and not without its difficulties - as most journeys are. Things can go wrong, especially with the unpredictability of different cultures and human nature.

It took them many days to reach their destination, and Ljuba —as the eldest of the flock—took on the role of protector and helped to shepherd his younger siblings on the long and arduous journey.

Ruth had booked seats in a train carriage, but some cheeky blighters had taken them without a by-your-leave. Ruth tried to explain the seats were hers, but they just kept saying they couldn't understand as they didn't speak English. Ruth and her children had to stand huddled up with their luggage around their legs on a very busy train - the discomfort of the journey is embedded in their memories to this day.

Hot and thirsty, when they reached a station, Ruth would send Ljuba to run and fill up water bottles while she watched him and kept an eye on the rest of her young family. But human compassion won in the end, and one kind gentleman who spoke a little English noticed how stressed Ruth was. He got the train inspector involved to sort out the problem, and he ensured their booked carriage was free for them to move into. From then on, that kind man and his family went to fill up their water bottles and gave them lots of chocolates to keep their energy up.

It was with great relief the train pulled into their final destination, where a massive crowd of people were waiting.

'They won't all get on this coach!' observed Ljuba.

But it turned out the crowd weren't there to get on the train - they were there waiting to greet them.

Ruth and the children received a right royal welcome.

It took a long time to walk to their grandmother's home because every house they passed on the way invited them in to have a drink and celebrate.

They were like pop stars and everyone made them so welcome even though the villagers had so very little.

There were no toilets at their grandmother's house, but their relatives had made them a shed without a door with a hole in the ground for Ruth and her family to use. Sounds of young Vera wailing wafted across the yard from the shed. She'd lost her shoe in the pit latrine. Ruth managed to retrieve it and clean it, but there was no way Vera was having that on her foot again.

Then, the smell of burning filled the air. Ljuba had set fire to the barn by smoking his cigarette there. Understandably, his grandmother became angry at him, giving him a thorough telling off and throwing a plank of wood at him.

Then, the sound of buzzing was carried on the breeze. Young Nicky had bashed into a beehive, releasing a swarm of angry bees swirling around the yard in a furious frenzy, adding to the chaos. Poor Vera got stung so much that she needed an injection, which didn't help as lots of itchy, painful bumps broke out.

Then, to top it all, the lads refused to pick the plums to help out.

'We are on holiday, why should we do it?' was their feeble excuse.

So it seems they were not such pop stars when they left, although plenty of people came to wave them off with tears streaming down their faces, crying because they were leaving - or maybe they were tears of joy, thinking, 'Thank goodness they're going home!'

It was an adventure of a lifetime for them all, with treasured memories of their father's relatives - an amazing experience, all made possible through Ruth's steadfast strength and courage.

My mother—who had her own brand of resilience—was amazed and in awe of her sister's bravery in undertaking such a task.

'Our Ruth, I can't believe it! Taking four children all that way!

What a thing to do. And to think they had to use a hole in the ground!'

But Chicka Mick eventually travelled to his home town many years later. His children got him British Nationalised before his 70th birthday, and this meant he was safe to go back to Serbia (former Yugoslavia). All four children put £200 towards the trip and bought him new clothes. He visited his old home for a few weeks, and although his mother and brother had died, he saw plenty of his family and had a wonderful time. We were all pleased that Chicka Mick got to go home and be reunited with his family over half a century after he'd left.

Visits to my cousins in Bloxwich opened up a whole new world for me. At the back of their house, a scrubby wasteland stretched out, and in summer, we would go and play there as it shimmered under the scorching summer sun. Pylons towered above us, their metallic hum blending with the sounds of our laughter. The air carried a faint scent of earth and dried grass as we hiked our way towards the rezza (reservoir), its murky waters reflecting the hazy sunlight. We'd take jam sandwiches and a bottle of squash, pretending we were at the seaside, ignoring the dirty brown water.

Amid our playful escapades, drab brown Hawker dragonflies would dart and buzz around us, their delicate wings creating a gentle whirring sound. Tommy and Nicky, always a tad mischievous, would seize the opportunity to tease me relentlessly, taunting me with misinformation that the dragonflies had stingers. They whispered tales that a single sting would cause a lump the size of a fist. Their words sent me running away from the critters. Even now, the sight of a dragonfly sends me scrambling indoors, seeking refuge from a fear deeply rooted in an irrational childhood belief.

The Mossley Estate, where they lived, had a rich and diverse community with a vibrant undercurrent. My grandmother and young Royston used to travel to Ruth's nearly every Friday evening, staying the whole weekend, and she always wanted to move house and live on 'The Mossley'. But Mossley also had what would today be called a sub-culture amongst the youth, and Ljuba would get into fights with the local neighbourhood kids because they wouldn't believe that Roy was his 'Uncle' - Roy being just three years older than Ljuba, and both of them wearing short trousers. But this protective behaviour of Ljuba was a trait all the brothers had and was one of the many reasons Ljuba was the closest Roy ever came to having a brother.

Ljuba loved cars, and as he grew older, he became a talented car mechanic, following in his grandfather's footsteps. One of the first vehicles he ever owned was an ancient, rickety Landrover that had no suspension. He once gave me a lift home in it, for he was adamant I wouldn't be travelling alone from Bloxwich to Northfield on public transport on a Saturday night. It was one of the most uncomfortable journeys I've ever been on - the vehicle was a right "boneshaker". But I've never forgotten Lju's kindness. There aren't many cousins who would do a 45-mile round trip on their day off.

My cousin Vera—a few years younger than myself—was a delightful annual visitor to our home during the summer holidays. With three boisterous brothers in her life, coming to stay at our house was certainly a different experience for her, and it was nice for me to have some company my age.

Coming from Walsall, all my cousins had strong Black Country accents, and my father especially enjoyed the difference in pronunciations and inflections peculiar to that part of the UK. He took great delight in getting Vera to say "how now brown cow" which she would consistently say in a Black Country accent, pronouncing the word "brown" as "brow-en". My father loved it. I also loved how Vera pronounced "shoes" - which came out as "shewez".

'Where's me shewez?' she would say.

We often made up our own fun, such as scaring my mother witless one night when she was having a bath. By stealth, we tapped the bathroom window by letting down an object from my bedroom window on a piece of string.

'Les! Les!' my mother called.

'What? What's wrong?' he responded, annoyed at having to stop watching *Til Death Do Us Part* to investigate the problem.

'Quick! There's someone outside the bathroom window, go and check.'

She was convinced it was a peeping tom.

The next morning we made footprints using my father's shoes behind the greenhouse to make believe someone had been around. Oh, how naughty.

If we had a few spare pennies, we'd eagerly make our way up to the Post Office in Northfield. There, four worn-out phone boxes greeted us, their paint peeling and fading. They had a peculiar and unique odour of stale cigarette smoke mingled with general musty, cold, damp, and decay.

We would eagerly call each other from adjacent phone boxes, the stink of metal and old coins wafting through the air as we pushed our money into the slot. With small fingers, we would delight in the tactile sensation of operating the stiff dials, relishing in the satisfying click and the sound of the rebound that echoed in our ears. Through the smudged glass of our phone booths, we would lock eyes, excitement dancing in the air between us. As we leaned into the heavy mouthpiece, the familiar pungent pong of musty plastic mingled with the lingering aroma of countless conversations before ours. We would speak into it, our voices carrying the weight of our carefully written words on a piece of paper. In that moment, we felt a sense of grown-up independence, as if we had unlocked a secret world of communication. Meanwhile, a restless queue of impatient people would often form, their murmurs and shuffling feet creating a background symphony, as they awaited their turn while we exchanged our carefully crafted words from our shared script. We soon got cut off from each other when our money ran out.

After our telephone escapade, we would saunter into Woolworths and have fun in the photo booth. This was a popular thing to do with other friends. A perfect way for 70s kids to have fun and acquire some 70s selfies.

FUN IN THE PHOTO BOOTH - 1974
With little sis (with the hat on) and friends
(nice shot of my fringe above my little sis's hat - it was
a squash with five of us in the booth.

Selfie with cousin Vera in Woolworth's photo booth

These family stories and memories are like images flashing through the mind - a tapestry of random recalls of this and that, but memories which pack a punch of atmosphere, fondness, warmth and happy times that cost nothing.

18. A WORKING-CLASS CHRISTMAS

'He's been, he's been, he's been!' cried my father in excitement as I sat up in bed and opened my Christmas stocking.

My father literally said, 'Is bin! Is bin! Is bin!' - "bin" being a popular Birmingham way of pronouncing "been", though sometimes this could be mixed up with a rubbish bin, as was the case when my mother—during her job as a hospital cleaner—asked a West Indian patient sitting up in her hospital bed, 'Where's yer bin?' whilst she searched for the bin to empty, but not finding it anywhere present.

'Ah's ain't bin nowhere, man!' was the reply, demonstrating that even fellow Brummies can sometimes get meanings mixed up! ...but I digress...

For nine years I believed that Father Christmas existed, and my father would always make his excited "is bin, is bin, is bin" call, and we'd then inspect the crumbs left over from the mince pie, the empty sherry glass and the letter from Father Christmas written in special curly writing thanking us for the refreshments.

We had a weedy silver Christmas tree that we'd put up year after year and decorate, draping it with scrawny tinsel and coloured lights to give a festive glow, not forgetting the customary fairy sitting atop. Our fairy had seen better days and had dilapidations, but we were very fond of her. The same battered advent calendar came out on the 1st of December each year too, and it got more and more dog-eared as the years went by.

My mother would meticulously hang cheap but vibrant trimmings made from soft crêpe paper, their colours spanning from one corner of the living room to the other, creating a mesmerising criss-cross pattern in the middle. Colourful concertina Chinese lanterns completed the festive look, hanging from the ceiling.

We always had turkey on Christmas Day, and roast pork with crispy crackling on Boxing Day, and those meals were made all the more special because my mother always made soup as a "starter". It felt very posh.

We also had other special foods augmenting the festive fare. The tantalising aroma of fresh ham would waft through the air, mingling with the rich pong of various strong cheeses, including the pungent blue cheese that my father adored.

My father, always wanting to make Christmas extra special, would buy a load of booze. Famous brands (only the best) of whisky, brandy, and rum were among his choices, each offering its own distinct aroma and character. The scent of Dubonnet, Port, Sherry, and Cherry Brandy would add a touch of sophistication to the air, and I was always allowed a Babycham, with an Opies cherry in.

These all sat on the "sideboard" well into January and sometimes February as my parents worked their way through the dregs. It was during this time that my parents savoured each drink, relishing the last drops of the bottles as if holding onto the memories of the holiday season.

Christmas was the only time that our drop leaf table was spread out full length with both wings up and laid over with a white cloth. It was moved into the centre of the living room and adorned, of course, with the obligatory Christmas crackers with their corny jokes, cheap plastic 'novelties' and paper hats which we all donned with aplomb - a tradition that remains today in the U.K. All these things gave our Christmas dinner a truly distinguished feel. My father never drank wine, but on Christmas Day, he would buy a bottle of white and have a small glass with my mother and a small sip for me - it was another small difference that gave Christmas significance.

One year in the mid-60s, my nan came to spend Christmas with us (it's the only time I ever remember her visiting our house before she became too infirm), but she ate so much that she ended up feeling ill and bloated, 'Oh! I'm so bloated. Oh dear! I feel so bloated,' she moaned half regretfully, half laughing, after consuming a super-large Christmas dinner, as she splayed out on the settee watching the Queen's speech. But the overriding lingering feeling of her visit was that my mother had been delighted to show her mother love by having her spend Christmas with us - a memory she cherished.

As working-class people were getting better wages, and cheaper goods made abroad began flooding the market, 60s children like myself benefitted and enjoyed Christmases with lots of presents - though not that we always appreciated it. When I was five, I came downstairs to a huge pile of Christmas gifts (which my mother had spent hours wrapping), only to announce after I'd opened them, 'Is that all?'

My mother told me this many years later and was somewhat shocked at my ungrateful comment. She was disappointed, to say the least.

My father would tell me every year how, as a child, all he'd had at Christmas was an orange, some tin toy soldiers, and a few nuts in a stocking, and maybe a new penny. He told me this without malice, and in one way with a degree of accomplishment that those days were now well and truly gone, and better times lay ahead for the working classes.

My mother would buy sweet treats such as Turkish Delight and candied orange and lemon slices. However, she never bought anything made from marzipan because my father hated the stuff. It was too sweet and sickly for him, and I shared his dislike of it.

"Nastypan", he called it.

Favourite television programmes adorned Christmas time, such as the (now politically incorrect) Black and White Minstrel Show, Benny Hill, Val Doonican, Andy Williams, and later comedy acts like Morecambe and Wise and The Two Ronnies. All these made for a jolly time, and the overriding aura of these wintery weeks was one of enjoyment and a break from the usual routine.

Compared to some of my friends, I was quite well off. I had two friends from larger Catholic families whose mothers were widows, and they didn't enjoy the good things I did at the best of times, let alone at Christmas. Their mothers had to work hard, money was tight, and a weekly evening meal might comprise just bread and lemon curd, having had a free school meal to fill their tummies earlier in the day. Their homes were sparse, and their Christmases, which only began after attending Mass on Christmas Day, were frugal and less prosperous. Of this, however, I was only mildly aware as we weren't into comparing our differences; it was only muted observations, noted from my friends' comments or the occasional visit to their homes, that I became aware of the disparity between us.

"Oh! the okey kokey! OH! the okey kokey! **OHH!** the okey kokey, knees bend, arms stretch, rah, rah, rah!"

At our neighbours the Lolley's, the tiny living room was bursting with vibrant sights and sounds packed with over a dozen people squeezed in for their annual Boxing Day buffet. The room was adorned with colourful decorations, with twinkling lights on the Christmas tree casting a warm glow. Laughter filled the air, intermingling with the delicious aroma of freshly prepared food.

"Bring out the Branston!" chanted my father, imitating the advert for Branston pickle, as he walked through the front door, his voice harmonising with the joyful atmosphere, the scent of Branston pickle wafting through the room adding a tangy twist to the festive ambience.

Piles of cheese and Branston pickle sandwiches, ham and mustard sandwiches, turkey and stuffing sandwiches, and cheese and onion cobs, alongside plates of sausage rolls and Scotch eggs, were spread out on the drop leaf table that had been spread full wing in the living room up against the back wall. Pyrex dishes full of salad, crisps, and nuts, together with a massive bowl of trifle and a marvellous Christmas cake, completed the feast.

As we manoeuvred around each other, balancing plates full of food on our laps, the room buzzed with excitement and anticipation. After our appetites were satisfied, the furniture was pushed aside, creating a makeshift dance floor. The room transformed into a lively spectacle as we all rose to our feet, tightly packed in a circle, joining in the energetic dance and infectious laughter. The sound of our footsteps reverberated through the room, adding to the rhythm of the "Okey Kokey" song. With each step, the floor creaked beneath us, and the warmth of the room enveloped us, causing beads of sweat to form on our foreheads. As we joyfully danced in and out of the circle, bending knees, shaking our legs about, stretching arms, shouting "Rah! Rah! Rah!", our inhibitions were laid aside, creating a sense of camaraderie and togetherness.

The Lolleys always gave me and my sister a sackful of presents - their generosity knew no bounds. They were more like relatives to us than neighbours.

Many years later, when it came to light that my father's real surname wasn't Smith, but Jolley (due to my grandfather changing his name at some point), everyone joked that if our families ever intermarried, they might adopt an unusual double-barrel name: Jolley-Lolley. Cool.

My mother, along with many other women of that era, would never take down the Christmas cards or decorations until the 6th of January. It was an old custom and those days between the 1st and 6th of January had an aura of sadness; the magic of Christmas was now a thing of the past, and the obsolete decorations were a reminder that it was gone for another year. It seems unthinkable nowadays when many people, including myself, take everything down on New Year's Day. Though conversely, decorations seem to go up in November or even October these days - something which would never have happened in the 60s and 70s.

Christmas for us and our close neighbours was a community affair with sharing and caring amongst us, forging a bond that strengthened the sense of belonging.

19. COLMERS FARM
SECONDARY MODERN

Having failed the Eleven Plus exam and after a family conflab, it was decided I'd go to Colmers Farm School in Rubery—a bus ride away—with my best friend Annette. Annette and I had become firm buddies at St Laurence Junior School, and she only lived around the corner from me, so we would travel to school together and come home together.

Norma went to Tinkers Farm school, which was much nearer, plus it was tempting to go to the same school as her, but being four years older than me, she would be leaving school in a year or two.

So Colmers Farm it was.

As it turned out, I thrived at Colmers and considering it was a secondary modern, it's my opinion and experience that I received a high standard of education there.

The school had a vibrant staff that motivated the pupils, particularly in practical subjects such as drama and music. For the boys, woodwork and technical drawing were on the curriculum, and for us girls, cookery and sewing. We were taught how to sew - both embroidery and machine. Embroidery classes inspired in me a love of crewel stitches - particularly using silk threads. We learnt blanket stitch and chain stitch first and then learnt more complex crewel stitches, such as satin stitch, and long and short stitch. But it was the French knots that I loved doing the best. My love of crewel embroidery continued after I left school, becoming a hobby that brought hours of pleasure for many years.

Close-up of one of my crewel embroideries - the centres
of the daisies are done with French knots.
It is thanks to my education at Colmers that my love of embroidery was nurtured.

I wasn't good at dressmaking, however, and my clothes always had a homespun look to them. I found using an electric sewing machine required coordination skills I didn't have.

'Miss!' I put my hand up as I attempted to machine stitch a seam in a skirt. 'Miss! There's something wrong with my sewing machine. It's scrunching up the material.'

Miss came over to inspect. She removed my crumpled garment out of the machine and sewed a different piece. The sewing machine worked perfectly, producing a beautifully smooth seam.

'It's not the machine, dear, it's you.'

I did improve a little, but try as I might, there were many puckerings or missed stitches in my feeble attempts. And buttonholes were a disaster.

Garments such as skirts, blouses, and trousers were made from patterns, and we were also taught how to iron a shirt correctly (yes, there is a particular method to it!).

Cookery was a different type of practical subject and I had more success with that.

On the day of the cookery lesson, our wicker panniers were packed full of ingredients our mothers had purchased for us, their weight pressing against our arms as we travelled to school. The classroom buzzed with activity as the victuals were transformed into a dish we could eat at home. We'd leave school with the finished product in our cookery baskets, filling the bus with enticing aromas. Simple English classic dishes such as apple charlotte, lemon meringue pie, cottage pie, and chicken pie were recipes that we learnt, amongst others.

However, I was once very naughty at school.

Spurred on by Sinead, one of my best friends, we decided to play truant - the idea lingering in the air like a mischievous whisper. I knew it was wrong and I'd never done it before, and I never did it again. But just the once, it was enticing. We were all afraid of the "wag man", but the chirruping birds and summer sunshine created an alluring backdrop to our daring adventure.

We decided to catch the number 62 bus to the Lickey Hills instead of the number 63 to Rubery that went to Colmers Farm school. The bus dropped us right at the foot of the Lickeys, and the earthy aroma of nature enticed us further. It was a beautiful day, and the lure of the hills beckoned, their slopes calling out to be explored. We felt as free as a bird roaming the length and breadth of the hills.

And then we saw it.

We came upon a magnificent house. It appeared out of nowhere, unexpectedly. I'd been to the Lickey Hills many times before but had never ventured upon this residence. It was vast and seemed like a palace to us, its grandeur captivating our young minds.

We walked around it, the soft crunch of gravel and stones beneath our feet echoing in the quiet surroundings. We were captivated by the mystery house. Who lived there? What were they like?

Then Sinead had a brain wave: we would knock on the door and ask for a donation of goods for a jumble sale we were collecting for. So we knocked, the sound reverberating through the stillness, eagerly waiting to see who would answer. Would they be friend or foe?

After a few minutes, a mature lady opened the door and listened patiently as we told her our cock-and-bull story, making our request for jumble sale items. She said that she hadn't got anything, but she gave us a 10p coin each instead for our cause, the clink of coins filling the air, like a small victory for our audacity and dishonesty. In our sweaty palms, the coins were cool, shiny and new, for Britain had not long converted to decimalisation*, and in our minds, the 10p pieces were worth 24 old pence, the equivalent of two shillings each. We felt rich.

What a gracious and trusting lady she had been, to believe our lie. Or maybe she didn't believe us. Maybe she just wanted to be kind and enjoyed being generous to two random young teens who'd had the gall to knock on her door.

We couldn't believe our luck. We were elated, our hearts pounding with excitement. Looking back, it was a risky thing we did - two girls out on the prowl, knocking on the door of strangers. It could have all ended rather badly. What if an evil person had lived there? It could have been a disaster.

But then we had to face the music the next day when we went to school. We would have to tell another lie to our Form Teacher about our absence. The smell of chalk and musty books filled the classroom creating an atmosphere of seriousness and discipline. Technically, we should have had a letter from our parents explaining our absenteeism. But that was impossible as neither of us could bring ourselves to ask our mother for such a letter. So we just winged it somehow, our nerves tingling with anticipation. My Form Teacher was Mr Walters, his voice firm yet kind as he listened to my fabricated story, 'I believe you, though thousands wouldn't,' he said. In that moment the room seemed to hold its breath with the weight of potential consequences hanging in the air. I think he was perhaps just being kind, or maybe he hadn't got the energy to pursue it, the sound of his voice carrying a hint of weariness.

It never happened again.

(In writing this memoir, I was curious google houses on the Lickey Hills, and learned that the house we stumbled upon was probably the Cadbury family mansion).

*Decimalisation in the UK occurred on 15 February 1971, when the currency system switched from having 240 'old' pence in the pound to having a 100 'new' pence in the pound. We were told it was to harmonise with international standards, but many British people felt cheated!

The Welsh Mr Davies was another interesting member of staff. He infused a musical ethos in the school, and it was due to his influence that I chose music as one of my O-level subjects.

There were five of us who opted to study music (I was the only girl), yet none of us could read a note. As enthusiastic as Mr Davies was about inspiring a love of classical music, he wasn't good at teaching the technicalities of it, and all five of us remained musically illiterate as the term wore on.

I was so frustrated I couldn't understand how to read music, I was on the verge of giving it up. If it hadn't been for the Deputy Head, Mr Vaughan, encouraging me to persevere with music, I would have packed it in as a subject.

Mr Davies was an ebullient character coming up to retirement. He shouted a lot during break times, pretending to be strict, and the pupils pretended to be scared of him.

'Stand over there and make a noise like a carrot!' was one of his frequent reprimands—delivered in his delightful Welsh brogue—to noisy pupils in the corridors.

I loved the lessons with him where we listened to classical music. I remember being blown away by the harpsichord solo in Bach's Brandenburg Concerto No. 6.

'It's brilliant, isn't it?' Mr Davies observed, to which we all heartily agreed. How was it even possible to play so many hundreds of notes so quickly, let alone make them sound a stunning delight to the ear? But our pleasure at listening did little to help our understanding of the theory of music, which remained very poor indeed.

Our musical fortune changed when our headmaster, Mr Ball, appointed an excellent part-time music teacher called Mrs Medhurst. Elegant, calm yet vibrant, she drove a sporty car (with the roof down in summer) and was accompanied by her beautiful Labrador and occasionally her young son. She took us—a bunch of music no-hopers—and, unfazed by our sheer inability, taught us the basics beginning with clapping out crotchets, minims, quavers and semi-breves.

Then she taught us the Tonic sol-fa (a bit like Maria taught the von Trapp children in *The Sound of Music,* though we didn't sing the "Do-Re-Mi" song. I guess getting a bunch of 16-year-olds to sing "Doe a deer" wouldn't have gone down that well!). But the Tonic sol-fa taught us about pitch. That skill has been a lifelong tool for me and clinched me a place as a soprano in the CBSO Chorus when I auditioned for the choir in 1980. The CBSO Chorus was a top-notch amateur choir that sang choral works with the world-renowned City of Birmingham Symphony Orchestra. I don't think I'd have got in just on my voice quality, but they were so impressed with my sight-singing where I used the Tonic sol-fa, I got a "bravo!" for it from the deputy choir master, Peter King, who conducted the audition, as well as a place in the choir.

Mrs Medhurst taught us how to write down music from dictation along with the complex rules of composing and four-part harmony. The O-level music syllabus was quite challenging in the 70s, but she made it a breeze.

She gave us a wonderful passion for classical music as we studied the set works for our O-level syllabus. Haydn's Creation (with John Shirley-Quirk as tenor - oh how I loved that name!) was one of my favourite works and my love of singing was cemented as we studied this beautiful choral piece. The technical coloratura brilliance of the soloists made my jaw drop and left me spellbound. How did they do it? They seemed like gods, with voices from another world.

Under her excellent tuition, we blossomed.

I can honestly say that if it hadn't been for Mr Vaughan's encouragement and Mrs Medhurst's excellent teaching, I would have given up music. I would never have enjoyed singing in choirs and would certainly never have become a hotel pianist.

A good teacher has the power to change lives.

But I had a problem. I was learning to play the piano but had no instrument to practice at home. Mr Ball came to my rescue and allowed me to practice the piano during lunchtime in the prefab music classroom, and he gave me special permission to have my lunch every day at the first sitting.

To enhance my practice further, I got one of my father's large newspapers, The Birmingham Post, and drew piano keys on it with a big blue marker pen. Then I laid it out on the table, and practised my scales, arpeggios and pieces on it, even though it made not a single sound. I could at least rehearse my fingering and familiarity with the notes.

My parents were moved to their core seeing me do this, and they cashed in an insurance policy (from the "Pru" of course) and bought me a second-hand upright Kemble Minx piano, which was duly delivered to our home. I was in music heaven with it, and having my own piano, there was no stopping me. I went from strength to strength. My mother found a private piano teacher, Joyce Warne, to take me through the higher grades.

Joyce was a wonderfully inspiring and nurturing teacher. Being a string player, she also encouraged me to learn the viola. She became like a mother to me, as she was to all her pupils, taking us under her wing and empowering us to achieve musical standards we never thought were possible. We did our best at music because we loved her.

I was blessed with the finest of music teachers.

My passion for singing began in Junior School and continued through to Secondary School where the Welsh Mr Davies formed a choir every Christmas and got some good singers to warble the David Wilcocks descants to *O Come All Ye Faithful* and other carols. I was bowled over by these descants where two different strands of music juxtaposed each other in a skin-tingling combination.

I was in love with choral singing.

It gave me goosebumps.

It's thanks to Mr Davies that I joined a choir in my late teens. I never forgot the buzz that singing with others gave me, and my love of choral singing was birthed by his perseverance in teaching a load of working-class kids to sing David Wilcocks descants - a task not for the faint-hearted. How he did it, I do not know. Quite a feat when I think about it now.

Secondary school was very much a driver for the fashion of the 70s era and Crombie coats, platform shoes, bell-bottomed trousers, maxi skirts (mini-skirts were out), tank tops, and blouses with long pointed collars and cuffs were all the rage. Some of these trends infiltrated through to the school uniform, with the girls sporting the latest fashions in the school colours.

Some odd behaviours became fads - such as scratching a word on our arms with a pin (forming a scabby tattoo) - a rather stupid thing to do which could have caused infections, but as it turned out, no one got ill. Thankfully, this craze didn't last very long. And, of course, everyone tried smoking a cigarette. This usually happened at the back entrance of Colmers. I tried one drag of a fag when I was 14, nearly choked, and never touched a cigarette again.

I left Colmers in June 1977 before moving on to higher education to study music later that year. I'd reached the dizzy heights of Head Girl and left with some profoundly affirming comments on my School Leaving Certificate.

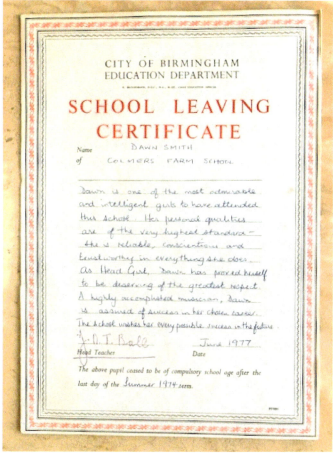

Would those comments have been written had they known about me playing truant?!

20. BOYS BOYS BOYS

'Bri-an! **BRI-AAAN!** Brian FOW-LER!' Norma yelled at the top of her voice cupping her mouth with her hands to make the sound go further.

We were standing on top of the rubbish dump at the bottom of my garden, which overlooked the allotments. Brian Fowler lived in the council houses across on the other side.

'What yer callin' 'im for?' I enquired.

'Cos I fancy 'im. D'yer know what that means?' she asked in a conspiratorial tone.

'Yeah, it means yer like 'im.'

'D'you know the facts of life?' enquired Norma in a subdued voice.

'No.'

'D'yer wanna know 'em?'

'Yeah, go on then.'

'All right,' and she proceeded to expound the most basic of biological facts of what body parts go where. It was all very matter-of-fact and quite interesting to my nine-year-old mind. And since Norma was thirteen and had already been two years at the "big school", it seemed quite natural she would know more about such things.

We then ate a packet of candy cigarettes (after pretending to smoke them), and Norma went home for tea. I promptly, and proudly, went and told my mother that I knew the facts of life.

'WHAT?! How?!' she demanded.

'Norma told me them.'

Clop, clop, clop went my mother's heels as she marched round to Mrs Lolley, with me in tow.

'Your Norma's just told our Dawn the facts of life and she's only nine!'

This outburst of confrontational behaviour was out of

character for my mother, for she was always very friendly and on exceptionally good terms with the neighbours; she loved them all. But this breach of trust by Mrs Lolley's daughter had caused a spike of brief anger, which soon dissipated when Mrs Lolley invited us in for a cuppa and cake.

'Well she's got to learn some time Barb, come on in luv, I'll put the kettle on. I've just baked some rock cakes.'

The incident was soon forgotten.

But in reality, boys weren't of that much interest to me or Norma particularly—we preferred to play Monopoly where we found untold pleasures in this boring and monotonous game, or listening to the Carpenters or Elvis; or when all the old fencing came down at the bottom of our gardens and were piled up on top of each other in the field, we played "Pirates" on the rickety wood. How we didn't have an accident or get tetanus from all the rusty nails, I'll never know, but we were good.

It wasn't until I went to Colmers Farm that boys became more of a thing, but even then, it was with a pinch of salt - particularly for me as I spent hours learning my music. I preferred the company of my beloved Kemble Minx piano rather than a boyfriend.

However—shock horror—often it wasn't the boys who chased and harassed the girls, it was the other way round at Colmers Farm. There was a very handsome young pupil called Brian Taylor whose father was a local butcher. At hometime, when Brian Taylor got off the bus opposite Kalamazoo Business Systems Ltd on the Bristol Road, the wicked girls sitting on the back row who fancied him would rhythmically chant in unison at the top of their voices for all to hear,

'Don't get playing with yer meat on the way 'ome Taylor!'

Brian's face turned blood red with embarrassment, but the girls were unrelenting. Meh...poor lad! I confess I did join in this awful chant on the odd occasion when I found myself sitting at the back of the bus with the gaggle of girls. But it was more the empowerment of the rhythmical chant than anything.

21. MONEY MONEY MONEY

'Come on, Dawn, shake a leg! I've made a milky coffee!' my mother called upstairs.

It was 1 p.m. and I was still in bed.

During the mid-70s, I got into a bad habit of getting up at lunchtime at weekends. I was a daydreamer and spent the morning making up stories and scenes in my head and creating imaginary friends.

I was 14 going on 15, and thoughts about my future were beginning to surface, and my ideas pipped to the post the sentiments enshrined in the comical Abba song "Money Money Money" (which was released in 1976).

In the song, the girl has dreams and plans to meet a wealthy man. She wouldn't have to work and could have a ball. But there's a problem: a man like that is hard to find, "ain't it sad?" And even if she did find such a man, would he be interested in her?

Before this song was released I'd hatched a plan to learn to drive as soon as I could, whisk myself off to the cocktail bar at the Chateau Impney Hotel in Droitwich, or become a croupier in a casino and meet a wealthy man who would, of course, fancy me, fall in love, marry me and we'd live happily ever after in one of those big detached houses I craved as a child. He'd buy me a Jaguar car, nice clothes and jewellery, and we'd have holidays all over the world…Oh, and I wouldn't have to work at all.

But the Abba song proved to be true: a man like that is hard to find, quite apart from anything else. It was a foolish dream of a working-class girl who liked nice things and wanted a posh home, posh car, posh clothes, and to enjoy life, but with no idea how to get on and get it for herself.

I was being silly. My sense of entitlement was misplaced.

Later that year, I abandoned my immature teenage ideas when I began a spiritual quest, birthed through R.E. (Religious

Education) lessons at Colmers Farm, and my mind was geared towards higher values, along with the other love in my life: music.

Good job too, as I'd have been crap as a croupier.

Seeking a deeper meaning to life more than money
My baptism, 1975, at Longbridge Baptist Church, Birmingham
with my parents and little sis
(Religious Education lessons at Colmers Farm inspired a spiritual
quest, steering me away from empty dreams and to face reality)

22. ASPIRATIONS AND TREPIDATIONS

'What's that doing there?' exclaimed Norma as we gazed at a random cauliflower on top of the desk in the classroom, wondering where on earth it had come from.

It was September 1977, and we'd turned up for our weekly night school class in "Elocution Lessons". We'd signed up for this class in the hope of eliminating our Birmingham accents, and there, on our desk, was a cauliflower (I kid you not). How it got to be there, we never found out. Maybe it was a bad omen because, after only two weeks, it was curtains for our elocution lessons as the teacher sadly announced that due to low numbers (aka me and Norma), the class would be closing as there weren't enough pupils to make it viable. *Drat.*

I'd always been conscious of my working-class background from a young age, and my Birmingham accent didn't help - I wanted to be rid of it. In time, I came to a truce with it and gave up trying to hide it. It is part of who I am. However, I never could hide it despite attempts to alter the inflections.

I'd often get comments ranging from "You're not from round here, are you?" Or "Is that a Birmingham accent I hear?" Or "My goodness, I thought you were quite posh until you opened your mouth!"

On the outside, I can sometimes look as if I belong to a higher social class, but when I open my mouth and speak, the incongruity of how I look and how I sound is too much for some people to bear, and they just have to point it out to me.

My working-class background was subconsciously priming me for the fact that I wasn't ever destined for a high-paid job. I had aspirations, but didn't know how to drive them forward. And I was no entrepreneur. It just wasn't my thing.

Since childhood, I had yearned to belong to a different class of people - to be more wealthy and have a nice detached house with a car, a telephone and a colour television.

Having grown up on a council estate during the 1960s, I became aware of class differences from a young age when one warm, sunny day in 1965, my mother accompanied me on a school trip to Twycross Zoo. The coach, full of excited school children, passed through the affluent suburb of Solihull, which was adorned with palatial detached houses stretching along wide leafy roads. Each home was different in design; they were capacious with ample driveways and were so very different from the diminutive council house boxes we lived in at Wasdale Road. I'd never seen anything like them before. These exclusive houses were elegant, beautiful, enticing...

'Can we live in a house like that, Mommy?' I asked with a mouthful of salad sandwich, too curious to want an answer before swallowing.

'No darling,' my mother said in her posh voice, 'those houses are only for rich people with lots of money.' *Drat and double drat.*

So that was it. Diversity in wealth was revealed to me in that moment, and an understanding of class differences became a vague awareness. But as I grew older, I became conscious that a more privileged lifestyle doesn't always guarantee happiness. I learnt this through my imagination and playful fantasies. I would pretend I was rich, living in a grand house with luxurious possessions, only for my imagination to lead me into some sad scenarios, teaching me that wealth isn't a warrant for fulfilment.

My parents instilled a strong work ethic, and I worked hard at my music and studied it for three years, aspiring to become a professional musician. But it was a job which proved impossible to attain, especially as I was 14 when I began learning to play the piano—much too late to pursue a career as a soloist, so I settled into a Civil Service job instead, ending up as a VAT Control Officer.

But that's another story...

POSTSCRIPT

THWACK!

As I walked up Corporation Street on my way to a job interview, I heard a heavy thud behind me. I turned around to see what it was: a brick on the floor.

Where did that come from?

I looked up to the top of the building I was passing. I could see men working on the roof.

Crikey, that was a close one.

Having nearly not been born four times, I nearly died when I was walking up Corporation Street, and a brick landed a foot behind me. I carried on, not giving it another thought.

But it could all have ended so differently if I'd been just one second later.

EPILOGUE

During the 60s, I recall my mother commenting now and again about various famous people who were "writing their memoirs". Back then, it seemed a very grand thing to do, reserved for the rich and famous.

That began to change slowly as more and more ordinary people began to pen their lives, some becoming best sellers.

I had an uneventful childhood, but it's given me great pleasure to revisit those days and look back at my family's life and acknowledge the good things we enjoyed in the simplicity of ordinariness.

It has also been good to write about my journey into adolescence. I've always been a bit of a late starter. A late developer. My dream of being a professional musician as a working-class kid seemed to slip away from me, but I got there in the end, albeit not quite as I had envisaged! As a solo pianist, playing at hotels and weddings has introduced me to genres I never anticipated enjoying. And my time as a chorister in the CBSO Chorus, led by Sir Simon Rattle, provided the incredible opportunity to sing beautiful classical choral works at a professional level with world-class conductors and soloists. I am immensely grateful for the musical education I received.

When I think about my grandparents and the hardship they lived through compared to the lives of their grandchildren and great-grandchildren, the disparity is clear. We all enjoy a degree of wealth and luxury far beyond what they could have ever imagined; our grandparents would be amazed to know that their descendents have travelled the world to faraway places such as the Caribbean, Hawaii, Taiwan, Iceland, America and Canada, to name but a few - places they could only ever dream of visiting (even if they'd wanted to), yet for their grandchildren these places as holiday destinations have become a reality with rising standards of education and wealth for those with working-class backgrounds.

WHAT HAPPENED NEXT?

After studying music for three years and then securing a low-grade job in the Civil Service as a Clerical Officer, I eventually ended up as a VAT Control Officer working for Customs and Excise. A job I struggled with on many levels. That story is told in my memoir "Confessions of a VAT Inspector" where I begin by relating a story from one of my VAT visits...

1. FARMERS AND PLUMBERS

'Does sheep semen have VAT on it?' asked the farmer as we made our way to the farmhouse where I'd be inspecting his VAT records. I wasn't sure if he was having me on or trying to wind me up, but I had to give him the benefit of the doubt,

'I'm not sure to be honest, but I'll find out and let you know,' I puffed, breathless from trying to keep up with his stride as I lugged my heavy briefcase over farmyard gunk in a pair of high heels and a pencil skirt. If only female officers were allowed to wear trousers.

'Are you selling sheep semen then?' I probed in an attempt to keep up the illusion that he was being serious. But he was serious.

'Not at the moment,' he picked up a stick and threw it across the yard for his sheep dog, 'but I'm thinking about it. I've got to try and make more money somehow.'

It had never even occurred to me that sheep semen could be sold at all, let alone be a source of lucrative revenue for the government, and I was clueless as to whether "back on my guard dog's ashes?' that I decided VAT Control was a bit of a strange job. Besides, who in their right mind would want to be a VAT inspector anyway? It's hardly the sort of job any young person would aspire to, unlike noble professions such as being a vet, or a doctor.

It was September 1989, and I was thirteen months into my VAT training in and around Birmingham learning something new every day. Every week I was visiting all kinds of different businesses and met a variety of business people who were so diverse that I began to believe I'd lived my 28 years of life on the planet like a hamster in a tiny cage. Becoming a VAT inspector broadened my whole vista of life by bringing me into contact with the trading community and showcasing a vibrant city throbbing with a multitude of industrious people and productive firms. It had opened up a panorama of the business world along with its opportunities, difficulties, struggles, successes and - where VAT was concerned, temptations...

ABOUT THE AUTHOR

Dawn Fallon

Dawn Fallon was born in Birmingham in 1959. After studying music, she graduated in 1980 but laid aside her musical ambitions when she entered the Civil Service. She met Don in 1992, married in 1994 and they have one son, Tim. They live in Torbay in Devon.

ACKNOWLEDGEMENT

Special thanks to my sister, Elizabeth Palethorpe, to my cousins Vera, Dave and Tony, and to my Uncle Roy for sharing some of their cherished memories.

My thanks to *Publish with Ant Press* for designing and formatting the cover. Amazing job! I'm very grateful.

Sincere thanks to all my wonderful *We Love Memoirs* early readers: Pat Ellis, Linda Ann Foster, Julie Haigh, Beth Haslam, Rebecca Hislop, Val Poore and Alison Ripley-Cubitt, Marian Quick, who all went above and beyond what I asked of them. If only I could gather all of you together and throw a big party to show my appreciation of your time and diligence in reading my manuscript.

Last, but not least, thanks to my husband, Don, for not only being a writer's widower as I spent hundreds of hours penning this childhood memoir, but also for encouraging me in writing all my books, and being such a brilliant agent telling everyone about them!

BOOKS BY THIS AUTHOR

Confessions Of A Vat Inspector

When Dawn Fallon abandons her ambitions to be a professional musician and becomes a Civil Servant little does she realise she would be given a job as a VAT Control Officer - a job she struggles with on many levels, but with the help and support of her senior colleagues, she achieves a promotion, though finds the job no less difficult.

The job brings her into contact with some bizarre situations and an interesting variety of business people. As she visits businesses to inspect their accounts for Value Added Tax purposes, researches whether sheep semen is taxable, grapples with solving why a busy Chinese takeaway is making a huge loss and struggles to understand double-entry bookkeeping, will it become a job for life? Or will she find a way to follow her passion for music?

Globetrotting With Disabled Don - From Cannes To The Caribbean With Wheelchairs And Walking Sticks

Driving on the wrong side of the road, an accident up the Alps, Force 10 storms, seasickness, being robbed of 200 euros, a brush with bats, blocked toilets and other mishaps...travelling with (or without) Don had its moments!

Dawn thought her journeys abroad were over when she

married Don. He flatly refused to fly. Surprisingly, plenty of opportunities to travel the globe by car, ferry, and cruise ship presented themselves.

Venturing to France with Don, who has spina bifida, family friend Geoff, who'd had a stroke, and four-year-old Tim, as well as 89-year-old Harold, certainly added an extra perspective.

Written with warmth and humour, this ten-part memoir spans over thirty years and touches on some of the challenges that wheelchair users and disabled people face, as well as Dawn's role as a carer.

Dawn has discovered that travelling with a disability is usually difficult, sometimes scary, and often funny.

Sam - The Busker's Dog

An entertaining and humorous read for any dog lover. This is a light-hearted story of a Cavalier King Charles Spaniel, his quirks and foibles, some of his canine friends, and his adventures out on the streets with his disabled busking master. Illustrated with over 150 photographs. The book is written in the dog's voice from a dog's eye view of the world - from Christmas to bus rides, from swimming to sleeping, from walkies to human quirks. It also explores the interesting Cavalier King Charles Spaniel breed of dog, as well as giving insights into life as a street musician.

Diary Of An Able Seaman - 1954: A Year Onboard Hms Warrior (R31)

Les records his daily life onboard the aircraft carrier HMS Warrior (R31) in 1954 when the ship was deployed to the Far East. He details his jobs, his recreations, his punishments, snippets of his personal life and life in general as an Able

Seaman in the Royal Navy in 1954. Les was given the diary by Commander J G Wells for doing some special task and he wrote in it almost every day, including his observations about the evacuation of refugees from North Vietnam in September 1954 in Operation Passage to Freedom. The book is illustrated throughout with relevant photographs and images.

A REQUEST...

Authors absolutely rely on our readers' reviews. We love them more than a glass of chilled wine on a summer's night beneath the stars.

If you enjoyed reading this book as much as I have enjoyed writing it, I'd be ever so grateful if you could leave an Amazon review, even if it's simply one sentence.

I also have an author page on **Facebook**, and am on **X** and **Instagram** - I'd love to hear from you if you'd like to get in touch.

And don't forget my Blog which has extra photos of my childhood, plus photos relating to my other books, including Don and Tim and their exploits - **Dawn Fallon Author Blog**.

THANK YOU!

WE LOVE MEMOIRS...

...and finally, if you love reading memoirs, please do join the wonderful We Love Memoirs community on Facebook. You can chat with the author and other memoir authors and readers by joining this fun and friendly Facebook group -
We Love Memoirs Facebook Group

Printed in Dunstable, United Kingdom